The Protestant Reformation

Third Revised Edition

Edited by

Lewis W. Spitz

Department of History
Stanford University

GINN PRESS

Printed in the United States of America

10 9 8 7 6 5 4 3

ISBN 0–536–57840–0
BA 7553

 GINN PRESS
160 Gould Street/Needham Heights, MA 02194
Simon & Schuster Higher Education Publishing Group

About the Author

Lewis W. Spitz, the editor of this volume, received his Ph.D. from Harvard University, and is the William R. Kenan Professor of History at Stanford University. Past President of the American Society for Reformation Research, the Central Renaissance Conference, and the American Society of Church History, he served as editor of *The Archive for Reformation History,* and on the Editorial Board of *The Journal of Modern History,* and other scholarly journals. Professor Spitz was Fulbright Professor at the Institute for European History in Mainz, Germany. He is the author of *Conrad Celtis, The German Arch Humanists; The Religious Renaissance of the German Humanists; Life in Two Worlds: A Biography of William Sihler; The Renaissance and Reformation Movements,* 2 volumes; *The Protestant Reformation 1517-1559;* editor of *Career of the Reformer, Luther's Works,* Vol. XXXIV; editor of *The Reformation—Basic Interpretations,* and co-editor of *Major Crises in Western Civilization.* On May 13, 1987, he was elected a fellow of the American Academy of Arts and Sciences. On January 5, 1990, he was honored with a Symposium for his Renaissance Scholarship by the Institute for Early Modern Studies and the Huntington Library. The papers will be published as a *Festschrift* dedicated to his scholarship in Renaissance Humanism.

FOREWORD

In this book the reader will find a series of statements made between the years 1501 and 1559, illustrating the ideas, beliefs, and sometimes the fates, of men and women who had come to share a profound discontent with the church as it then existed and a positive determination to put new strength into the life of the spirit. They did not often agree on anything else; many times they denounced each other's theories and behavior, and sometimes even killed each other, although more often they met with violence at the hands of the established authorities. Except for Erasmus, the reforming humanist who stayed within the church, all of these people were "Protestants" on the offensive. As Professor Spitz points out, there had long been many Catholics who felt similar discontent and a similar determination, but their opportunity to launch a counter-offensive did not arise until the second half of the same century.

The spectrum ranges from Erasmus and Hutten the humanists, to Luther and Melanchthon; thence to Zwingli, to Sattler the Anabaptist and Servetus the Unitarian, to Calvin the theologian and lawgiver; and, finally, to the English reformers, a special breed—from the rabble-rousing Fish to Cromwell the administrator, Starkey the moderate, the King, and the Archbishop of Canterbury.

What did these people believe? Here we may read all of Luther's Ninety-five Theses, all of Zwingli's Sixty-seven Articles, the Anabaptist Confession, Farel and Calvin's Geneva Convention, Henry VIII's Six Articles, the Elizabethan Act of Settlement. *How did they reach their beliefs?* Here is the record of Luther's inner wrestling and theological break-through; here is Calvin's own account of his conversion. And here we may listen to the moving voices of human beings in the grip of passionate emotions: Melanchthon lamenting Luther, whom he ranks with Isaiah, John the Baptist, St. Paul, and

v

Augustine, and whom he remembers not only as a brilliant expositor and tireless fighter but as kind, affable, and gracious; Michael Sattler facing his judges' sneers and abuse as calmly as he faces their grisly tortures; Lady Jane Grey showing herself a Protestant theologian at age sixteen, four days before the authorities executed her.

By his choice of little-known documents to accompany the key central statements of the reformers, by his terse and lucid remarks prefaced to each selection, and by his sweeping, tightly-packed introduction to the whole volume, Professor Spitz has made it possible to see the Protestant Reformation vividly and to see it whole.

Robert Lee Wolff
Coolidge Professor of History
Harvard University

CONTENTS

IV. CALVIN'S ECCLESIASTICAL REFORM

V. THE ENGLISH REFORMATION

Introduction

"We have become the spectacle of the world," Luther once complained, and so he and the other religious reformers have remained. Although it is no longer fashionable for historians to speak, as did James Froude, of the Reformation as "the hinge on which all modern history turns," the great religious movement of the sixteenth century created events whose impact is still felt today and gave birth to ideas which are very much a part of the contemporary world. That movement toward reform and renewal within Christendom was primarily religious in its concerns and consequently highly theological in its expressions. "The deepest theme in history," wrote Goethe, "has been posed by the conflict between faith and unfaith." Because the Reformation focused in its religious dimension upon questions touching the most inward reaches of the human spirit, its historical era has remained of vital interest to western man. The eyes of the world are still upon the reformers, all the more so in our ecumenical age.

The division between Protestant and Catholic Reformation writings in this series is made for convenience only, for beyond the polemics and antithetical positions of both sides lay a common drive toward a revitalized spiritual culture which was in evidence before Luther's reforming activities began and lasted beyond his death. During the first four decades after the dramatic publication of the Ninety-five Theses in 1517, the evangelical movement and the reformed churches were on the offensive. The Peace of Augsburg in 1555 legalized the position of the Lutheran churches in the Empire and the Elizabethan Settlement of 1559 guaranteed the Anglican establishment. Calvinism was still embattled in France, but the North was firmly Protestant while Italy and Spain remained fairly securely Catholic. There followed then the final sessions of the Council of Trent and a resurgent Catholicism which kept Protestantism on the defensive for the remainder of the century. The writings in this volume are all taken from these first decades of the Protestant Reformation.

The reformers usually referred to themselves as the evangelicals and conceived of their religious communities as parts of the one holy universal or Catholic Church on earth. Only in later years was the term Protestant applied to the reformed or evangelical churches, and it was not until the seventeenth century that the Reformed and Lutheran Churches were defined and designated as separate church bodies. The term Protestant derived from the protest made at the Diet of Speyer in 1529 when the evangelical estates —princes and cities—objected to the decree that the religious *status quo* was to be preserved, no innovations introduced in additional territories, and that the mass should be everywhere tolerated. Although in sixteenth-century usage the word protest meant assertive affirmation as well as articulate objection, historians have often stressed the negative aspect, interpreting the Reformation primarily as a reaction against abuses and institutional decay. This view of the Reformation, popular with many nineteenth-century historians, stressed the moral decline of the clergy, the institutional corruption of the Church, and the displacement of the true spiritual ends by economic considerations and political power drives on the part of the ecclesiastical hierarchy.

That grave ills were spreading through the body of Christendom was widely recognized both by the churchmen and by lay critics as well. As early as 1215 the mighty Pope Innocent III charged the Fourth Lateran Council with achieving reform. As late as 1522 Pope Adrian VI instructed the legate Chierigati to confess to the Diet at Nuremberg:

> God has let this persecution of His Church occur because of men and especially because of the sins of the priests and prelates. The Holy Scriptures loudly proclaim that the sins of the people have their origin in the sins of the religious leaders. We know all too well that also in the case of this Holy See for many years many reprehensible things have taken place: abuses in spiritual things, breaking of the commandments, yes, that everything has taken a turn for the very worst! We therefore have no cause to wonder that the disease has been transplanted from the head to the members, from the popes to the prelates.

"We perceive a certain fatal change in human affairs," wrote Erasmus apprehensively. Popular preachers, monkish moralizers, and humanist critics joined an ever louder chorus of assault upon the abuses in the Church and cried out for reform "in head and members." Some, such as the Florentine historian Francesco Guicciardini, singled out the Roman See, as when he wrote with such Renaissance popes as Alexander VI, Innocent VIII, and Julius II in mind: "So much evil cannot be said of the Roman Curia that more does not deserve to be said of it, for it is an infamy, an example of all the shame and wickedness of the world."

During the closing centuries of the Middle Ages the Church was experiencing grave financial difficulties. Having adapted its organization to a feudal social and economic system, it was awkwardly trying to adjust its cumbersome institutional machinery to the developing capitalist system rapidly rising, especially in the economically more advanced city-states and territories in central and western Europe. The increased centralization of authority in the Church, the growing demands upon the Church for an ever greater number of judicial and administrative services, and the cost of the long and losing struggle with the rising national monarchies made new sources of income imperative for the Curia. But the increasing simony (illicit buying and selling of Church offices), nepotism (favoritism in making ecclesiastical appointments), and such gross excesses as the collection of annates (the first year's revenue from a benefice) and of reservations (taking payments for nominations to vacant benefices) all laid the Church open to charges of venality and immorality. When the element of a nascent nationalistic resentment against Italians and the Roman Church on the part of the Northerners was added, a very explosive situation had come into being. Erasmus wrote of the common *odium Romani nominis,* hatred of the Roman name, found in German cities. Revolutions are not so much created by revolutionaries as they are let loose by them. The revolutionary fervor in the expression of grievances and protests against exploitation was evident in writings of humanists such as Ulrich von Hutten, publicists such as Simon Fish, and reformers such as Luther. "God has given us," said Erasmus of Luther, "a radical physician."

The century and a half preceding the beginning of the Reformation saw a marked increase of religious fervor among the people in northern Europe. The external evidences of such a rise in popular piety are manifold, including the formation of brotherhoods, pilgrimages, endowments of benefices, publication of devotional works, and a multiplication of religious houses and even of heretical groups. The comprehensive dissatisfaction with formal Church life was largely the disappointment of the ardent lover. The formalism of ritual and religious exercises, the routine externalization or despiritualization of the sacraments, the pedantry and quibbling of scholastic theology, and the use of the ban—an extension of the office of the keys—as an instrument for sacerdotal or priestly domination, all offended a generation of men whose expectations and desires for spiritual nourishment were rising.

The response to abuses and to the spiritual deficiencies of the Church during the last centuries of the medieval period had taken various forms. There were the sharp critics of the Church such as Marsiglio of Padua (d. 1342) who was once a canon of the Cathedral in Padua and rector of the University of Paris. He turned against the papacy and became the author of the *Defensor Pacis* (1324) which made a frontal attack on ecclesiastical failings. John Wycliffe (d. 1384), a reformer and biblical translator in England, worked out theories of spiritual dominion which proved to be of great value to the English monarch seeking grounds for greater independence from the Roman See. John Hus (d. 1415), a professor at the University of Prague and leader of a reform movement in Bohemia, and Savonarola (d. 1498), the Dominican moralistic and ecstatic preacher in Florence, were also labelled "reformers before the Reformation" by nineteenth-century bourgeois historians interested in demonstrating gradualism and continuity in historical developments.

There were, secondly, the mystics who reacted to the rationalistic emphases in theology and to the externalization of Church life by stressing the inwardness of religious experience and the priority of true devotion over outer forms or dogmatic definitions. The range of late medieval mysticism was very great, from the highly intellectual Neoplatonic mysticism of the Dominican Master Eckhardt (d. 1327) in the Rhineland to the practical voluntaristic mysticism of the Brethren of the Common Life predominantly in the Netherlands as reflected in Thomas à Kempis' (d. 1471) *Imitation of Christ*. But by its very nature mysticism could not of itself be revolutionary.

Finally, there were the conciliarists who reacted to the Avignonese papacy and the subsequent papal schism by urging the priority of the universal councils over the papacy and calling for frequent meetings of such councils where all the orders in the Church would be represented. The leaders of conciliarism such as Pierre d'Ailly (d. 1420) and Jean Gerson (d. 1429) of the University of

Paris, represented both a reforming zeal and a mystical religious inwardness. Their efforts at Pisa (1409), Constance (1414-1418), and Basel (1431-1449) were not successful, for in 1460 Pope Pius II in his bull *Execrabilis* pronounced appeals to the council over the head of the pope heretical. But the conciliar idea did not die out and was appealed to by a few Catholics as well as by the Protestants during the period of the Reformation prior to the Council of Trent (1545-1563). These medieval reformers, mystics, and conciliarists had positive emphases of their own and were not merely reacting against the lowly state of Christendom, but their programs are more meaningful when seen against the general background of decline and dissolution in the life of the Church itself.

Renaissance humanism made its contribution not merely to a cultural efflorescence but also to a religious refinement both in Italy and in the North. Italian humanism tended toward an increasing inwardness and individualism in religious life which resulted in a spiritualization of the sacraments and of all institutional aspects of Church life. On one level this personalization of religion involved an emphasis upon the virtuous life of the individual informed by Stoic moralism. On another level the spiritualization of religion was carried so far, as in Marsiglio Ficino's (d. 1499) *Theologia Platonica* and Giovanni Pico's (d. 1494) *Conclusiones,* as to seek new sources of ancient authority and inspiration in Neoplatonic and Hermetic sources of pristine Christianity, the early patristic writings and Holy Scriptures themselves. Erasmus (1469-1536), the great prince of the Northern humanists, was dedicated to a *restitutio Christianismi.* The restoration of Christianity which Erasmus envisioned was to be achieved through a return to the pure fountains of Christian teaching. With this program in mind he devoted his scholarly career to editing the Greek and Latin church fathers and the New Testament itself. Even his more popular writings, while cuttingly critical of the low moral estate of the clergy, of superstitious practices, and of barbarous scholasticism, were intended to further his positive program of respiritualizing religious life by stressing the inwardness of faith, the simplicity of the evangelical precepts, and the imitation of Christ the Founder. In the *Enchiridion,* a handbook of Christian piety, he wished to combat the common error of making religion consist of ceremonies and, expanding on the Pauline theme "the letter killeth but the spirit maketh alive," he pleaded for the inwardness of true spiritual life. Later in the century Ignatius Loyola was to say that he froze when he read sections of this *Enchiridion*, for it lacked the fervor of true devotion. The Reformation was to be the work not of cool Erasmus but of Luther, a man of heroic faith, who combined in his own person both major spiritual forces of the century—the discontent with conditions in the Church and the desire for a radically new spiritual rebirth.

The Reformation began in a university setting and shared many features of the learned Renaissance humanist tradition. The expectation of a golden age was present at the outset. "We are at the dawn of a new era!" exclaimed Luther. The drive back to the sources (*ad fontes*) of Christian antiquity led to a greater appreciation of the ancient languages over the Latin of the Vulgate, of rhetoric over dialectic, of old authorities over late authors, of the early Church over the papal Church, and of the Word of God over all opinions and decrees of men. Francis Bacon noted this formal affinity of the Reformation and Renaissance humanism when he wrote in his *Advancement of Learning*, Book One:

> Martin Luther, conducted (no doubt) by a higher providence, but in discourse of reason finding what a providence he had undertaken against the Bishop of Rome and the degenerate traditions of the Church, and finding his own solitude, being no ways aided by the opinions of his own time, was enforced to awake all antiquity, and to call former times to his succours to make a party against the present time.

But in one essential way the Reformation differed from Renaissance humanism in even its religious dimension and that was in the intensity and depth of its theological concern. In his struggle for faith in a God of peace and mercy, Luther wrestled more desperately than did Erasmus with the problem of sin as man's basic alienation from God and of grace as man's complete restoration to the favor of God through faith in Christ. His rediscovery of the historical core of Christianity came by way of an evangelical insight into the meaning of a phrase in St. Paul's *Epistle to The Romans* while Luther was preparing his exegetical lectures during the academic year 1515-1516. The passage was Romans 1:17, "For therein is the righteousness of God revealed from faith to faith: as it is written, the just shall live by faith." Years later Luther recalled the nature of this theological breakthrough: "I pondered night and day until I understood the connection between the justice of God and the sentence 'The just shall live by His faith.' Then I grasped that the justice of God is the righteousness by which through grace and pure mercy, God justifies us through faith. Immediately I felt that I had been reborn and that I had passed through wide open doors into Paradise!" This experience of salvation by God's grace alone, bestowed upon man as a gift through faith without dependence upon human merits, became the touchstone by which Luther was to judge all religious practices and all church teachings, whether in the area of indulgences, sacraments, ceremonies, or dogmatic definitions. His entire career was devoted to the defense and promotion of this gospel or good news of salvation. "My affair is not a joint program," declared Luther. His exclusive interest was in the religious and theological reform of the Church, proclaiming the "promises of God and the benefits of Christ." That the Reformation movement involved matters of social, economic and political import was clear also to Luther, but these were not central to his concern.

Cardinal John Henry Newman, an English theologian and man of letters in the nineteenth century, argued that God affects history inside of man, changing his heart and so indirectly affecting history. At least in the history of the Reformation the initial phases of the movement seem to have followed upon changes within men of unusual religious sensitivity. Ulrich Zwingli (1484-1531), the reformer in Zurich, arrived at his evangelical view of Christianity independently of Luther but about the same time. His understanding of all the implications of this view continued to deepen until around the middle of 1520, as he slowly freed himself from Erasmian Christocentrism and his *Christianismus renascens* and developed a firmer hold upon Pauline Christology. As in the case of Luther, Zwingli's reformation derived from a new understanding of the Biblical message of God's judgment and God's grace. His acceptance of St. Paul's view of man and of the principle of Scriptural authority, and his experience of the presence of Christ indwelling in man served as the basis for his reform of German Switzerland. When he began his duties as peoples' priest in the Great Minster in Zurich on January 1, 1519, he moved into a position of tremendous influence for the reform of the Swiss Church. As an eloquent preacher and renowned patriot he exercised a powerful and decisive influence upon the city council and the people. The favorable response to the *First Disputation* of 1523 demonstrated the popularity of his program. His influence quickly spread to other cantons and beyond Switzerland and lasted in the Reformed churches long after his death in battle with the Catholic cantons at Kappel.

One measure of Zwingli's rhetorical impact and persuasive power was the influence he had in awakening to religious concerns a group of men in Zurich who took seriously the duty of searching the Scriptures independently of tradition and authority. Conrad Grebel, a man of humanist learning, became the founder of the Swiss Brethren and performed the first adult baptism in 1525 when he baptized, or rebaptized, George Blaurock in the house of Felix Manz in Zurich. These left-wing radicals (in Luther's day they were referred to as right-wing) saw no prospect for the reform of the whole body of Christendom. They urged rather a voluntary Church whose members, their sanctification symbolized by adult baptism, would withdraw from the papal or territorial church, would separate themselves as a church group from the state (in many cases refusing to take oaths before magistrates), and would seek religious liberty from all external restraints. The movement was joined by countless common folk who proved in most cases to be models of personal piety and devotion, nonviolent, and evangelical. But these "step-children" of the Reformation were considered by the magisterial reformers such as Zwingli to be heretical and by the magistrates to be subversive and revolutionary. They were heartlessly hunted down and persecuted. Their cause came into even greater disrepute as a result of the tragic attempt by Anabaptist leaders to set up a "heavenly Jerusalem" in the German city of Münster, 1534-1535. Fanatical leaders from the lower Rhinelands, which had been the seedbed of many heretical sects in the Late Middle Ages, seized the city, drove out the bishop and conservative elements, and attempted to create a primitive communist society, including the introduction of polygamy. This mad adventure brought a deeper cloud over the movement and it took decades under the leadership of men such as Menno Simons (1496-1561), a moderate Dutch Anabaptist, before Anabaptism gained general respectability in the eyes of rulers and people.

Two other generic types of "radicals" in addition to the Anabaptists emerged out of the turmoil of the Reformation. These were the spiritualists who stressed personal piety through the indwelling of the Holy Spirit and the evangelical rationalists who questioned the reasonableness of traditional dogmatic formulations of such concepts as the Trinity. They contributed more than others to the growth of religious toleration. The Lutheran spiritualist Sebastian Franck, for example, wrote in his *Chronicle:* "The Anabaptists are not entirely right nor is anyone else and from each we should take the best." The evangelical rationalist Sebastian Castellio (d. 1563) in his *Concerning Heretics* decried persecution of the Anabaptists with these words: "They were miserably slain, even those who were not in arms and what is still more cruel the suppression was carried on not only by the sword but also in books which reach farther and last longer, or rather forever perpetuate this savagery." In establishing religious pluralism Protestantism took the first major step toward toleration for minority groups. But the notion that uniformity of church practice was necessary for peace within a given political entity persisted with attendant government persecution of dissenters. The development of true toleration and genuine religious freedom required much cultivation and many heroic deeds of resistance. For the sixteenth and much of the seventeenth centuries the principle of *cuius regio eius religio* remained the rule.

For the evangelical churches the execution of Michael Servetus (1511-1553) in Geneva for heresy and subversion posed the question of religious liberty in a dramatic and tragic manner. In the words of the American church historian Roland Bainton, Servetus has the singular distinction of having been burned by the Catholics in effigy and by the Protestants in actuality. Born in Spain as the son of a royal notary, Servetus studied law and later medicine, his name being associated with the modern understanding of the pulmonary circulation of the blood. His legal, medical, and particularly his theological interests carried him to many parts of Europe, to Toulouse, Bologna, Basel, Strassburg, Paris, Lyons, and finally to Geneva. At the age of twenty this precocious but also obstinate and conceited young man gained a lasting reputation for religious deviationism with his treatise *On the Errors of the Trinity* in which he accused traditional scholastic theology of introducing Greek philosophical terms and non-biblical categories into the definitions of the Trinity. His own formulations were viewed by the Orthodox Catholics and many Protestants as constituting the reassertion of the ancient heresy of Arianism. In the year 1553 upon the publication of the even more radical *Restoration of Christianity* he was condemned by the Inquisition in Lyons. He escaped, but unhappily passed through Geneva on the way to Naples. In Geneva he was recognized, brought to trial, condemned to death by a state court, and burned at the stake on October 27, 1553. The revulsion against the severity of the punishment was very great. An Italian liberal Sebastian Castellio wrote his famous plea for toleration, *Concerning Heretics Whether They are to be Persecuted and How They are to be Treated.* The martyrdom of Servetus, the victim of a mistaken zeal for truth on the part of John Calvin and the Genevans, contributed tremendously to the growth of the ideas of religious toleration and liberty.

The thundering Scot, John Knox, wrote in 1556 of Calvin's Geneva: "Whair I nether feir nor eschame to say is the nearest perfyt school of Chryst that ever was in the erth since the dayis of the Apostillis." John Calvin was a mere boy of eight when Luther initiated the Reformation in Wittenberg. Destined by his father for the law, he developed into a young French humanist, experienced an evangelical conversion, and was against his will drawn into the maelstrom of the Reformation as the acknowledged leader of Protestantism in Western Europe and the strategist of its second militant phase. The historian D'Aubigné called Calvin "the legislator of the renovated Church." With a genius for organization he developed in Geneva that form of church government which became a model for presbyterian polity, a form which could maintain itself even in countries where the monarch and establishment might be hostile. Calvin was a man of frail body but iron will with a prodigious capacity for labor. His correspondence alone would fill thirty-five folio volumes, letters of reply to opponents like Cardinal Sadoleto, letters of encouragement to evangelical missionaries such as the martyrs of Lyons. In 1556, one of his followers, François Hotman, wrote to Calvin that in Geneva was engendered that spirit which raised up a new race of "martyrs in Gaul, whose blood is the testimony of thy doctrine and thy Church."

Melanchthon, Luther's young colleague on the faculty at Wittenberg, referred to Calvin as *ille theologus, the* theologian. He was, like Dr. Samuel Johnson, a man born to grapple with libraries, and his own works in translation comprise more than fifty volumes. But his most epochal work was the *Institutes of the Christian Religion* which stands out in religious literature as do Newton's *Principia* or Kant's *Critique* in science and philosophy. A "masterpiece of luminous argument," the *Institutes* were a clear, tightly-organized, and compactly-stated handbook of Christian doctrine which served as a weapon of defense and an implement for building in the cause of Calvinism. For a full appreciation of Calvin's work as a theologian, however, the student must read widely in his sermons and Biblical commentaries to understand fully his emphasis upon God's love for man and the nature of the sanctified life. To see no farther than his predestinarian doctrine is not to appreciate the Reformer very thoroughly. Before his death in 1564 he asked that he be buried in an anonymous grave, but his name will never be forgotten. "To omit Calvin from the forces of Western evolution," wrote the British author and statesman John Morley, "is to read history with one eye shut."

Protestantism was as varied in points of origin as it was in culture and dogma, emerging in a university setting, expanding outward from prosperous Swiss commercial cities, capturing feudal areas like Scotland, and winning a kingdom in the heart of the royal court of England. The story of the English Reformation has been told so often in terms of the "King's great question" that the religious concerns of England's earliest Protestants have not received the attention they deserve. During the Catholic or conservative phase of the Henrican reformation, a corps of evangelical reformers developed a body of religious ideas which were established during the reign of Protestant King Edward VI, preserved through persecution under "bloody" Queen Mary, and definitively enthroned legally and by long usage under Queen Elizabeth.

There is some truth in the Scottish historian and philosopher David Hume's Whiggish assessment of the English Reformation as the *via media* between papalism and radicalism when he wrote in his *History of England:*

> Of all the European churches which shook off the yoke of papal authority, no one proceeded with so much reason and moderation as the Church of England; an advantage which had derived partly from

the gradual and slow steps by which the Reformation was conducted in that kingdom. Rage and animosity against the Catholic religion was as little indulged as could be supposed in such a revolution.

Rage and animosity there were, and more to come in the century of the Civil War which followed, but there were also counsels of moderation such as Thomas Starkey's admirable admonition to unity and obedience. If Thomas Cromwell, Thomas Cranmer, and the other English reformers were not theological giants and creative geniuses such as Luther, Melanchthon, Zwingli, or Calvin, they nevertheless gradually evolved an evangelical consensus on matters of doctrine and church polity which became the theological superstructure of the Church in and of England.

Thomas Carlyle, the colorful Scottish essayist and historian, was obviously exaggerating when he wrote: "Protestantism is the grand root from which our whole subsequent European History branches out." Such a tribute belongs rather to Christendom as a whole. But it is also true that the Reformation in religion left few other areas of life completely untouched. Worldly society was to the reformers, to use Luther's phrase, "the sphere of faith's works." A Christendom which entered the era nominally unified under a single spiritual head and a single temporal ruler emerged as a Europe of particular territorial and national states and plural religious beliefs. The Reformation with its conception of the Church as a communion of saints and a community based on love rather than power and coercion forced men to reconsider the old theories of the relationship of Church and state. The doctrine of the priesthood of all believers and the stress upon direct personal access to the Scriptures led to a call for popular education to the point of universal literacy. The appreciation of the ancient languages, rhetoric, and history inherited from Renaissance humanism enthroned the classical curriculum. The role of the teacher was considered to be a special divine calling. The reformers transcended the medieval dualism of the sacred and the secular callings and raised the natural order to a new dignity. The importance of divine vocation to earthly tasks was of enormous significance for subsequent social and economic history in ways both direct and subtle. It is easy to fault Montesquieu, Voltaire, the other philosophes and the nineteenth-century liberal historians for assessing the importance of the Reformation largely in terms of these by-products. But the reformers themselves took man's involvement in society and in higher culture seriously as a *negotium cum deo,* a business to be carried on and looked after as co-workers with God.

The Reformation was above all an age of faith and of men willing to live by and die for their faith. The best historical sources from such an era are testimonies rather than mere traces. As the first major historical movement of the post-Gutenberg era the Reformation produced an imposing volume of such documents. Hopefully the selections which are offered here will illustrate the essential nature of the movement, the community of beliefs, as well as the varying emphases in the different Protestant traditions. The reformers would all agree to the tremendous importance of the task today's student undertakes in seeking to understand the past and to repossess his heritage. All would support Luther's declaration:

"The prosperity of a country depends, not on the abundance of its revenue, nor on the strength of its fortifications, nor on the beauty of its public buildings, but it consists in the number of cultivated citizens, in its men of education, enlightenment and character."

Part One

 THE HUMANIST CRITICS

1. Erasmus: The Praise of Folly

It is ironic that Erasmus, the greatest scholar among the northern humanists and the literary arbiter of his age, should be best known for *The Praise of Folly*, which has been published in over six hundred editions through the centuries. Compared with his scholarly editions of the Greek and Latin Church fathers and his more learned treatises it was a light satirical work which he dashed off in 1509 while resting from his Italian journey in the home of Sir Thomas More. Yet the *Folly* had the same serious purpose as his other works: to criticize abuses in the church and in society and to promote greater inwardness and purer spirituality in religion. The selections which follow present some of the most famous passages of the *Folly*, ridiculing superstition and idle ceremonies, castigating the insincere monks and the prelates and popes who bring shame upon their high office through impure and unchristian lives. In the preface to More he wrote, "We have praised folly not quite foolishly." From Desiderius Erasmus, *The Praise of Folly* (London: Hamilton, Adams, & Co., 1887), pp. 90-96, 143-149, 164-169.

The next to be placed among the regiment of fools are such as make a trade of telling or inquiring after incredible stories of miracles and prodigies. Never doubting that a lie will choke them, they will muster up a thousand several strange relations of spirits, ghosts, apparitions, raising of the devil, and such like bugbears of superstition; which the farther they are from being probably true, the more greedily they are swallowed, and the more devoutly believed. And these absurdities do not only bring an empty pleasure and cheap divertisement, but they are a good trade and procure a comfortable income to such priests and friars as by this craft get their gain.

To these again are nearly related such others as attribute strange virtues to the shrines and images of saints and martyrs, and so would make their credulous proselytes believe that if they pay their devotion to St. Christopher in the morning, they shall be guarded and secured the day following from all dangers and misfortunes. If soldiers, when they first take arms, shall come and mumble over such a set prayer before the picture of St. Barbara, they shall return safe from all engagements. Or if any pray to Erasmus on such particular holidays, with the ceremony of wax candles and other fopperies, he shall in a short time be rewarded with a plentiful increase of wealth and riches. The Christians have now their gigantic St. George, as well as the pagans had their Hercules; they paint the saint on horseback, and drawing the horse in splendid trappings, very gloriously accoutred, they scarce refrain in a literal sense from worshipping the very beast.

What shall I say of such as cry up and maintain the cheat of pardons and indulgences? That by these compute the time of each soul's residence in purgatory, and assign them a longer or shorter continuance, according as they purchase more or fewer of these paltry pardons and saleable exemptions? Or what can be said bad enough of others, who pretend that by the force of such magical charms, or by the fumbling over their beads in the rehearsal of such and such petitions; which some religious imposters invented, either for diversion, or, what is more likely, for advantage; they shall procure riches, honor, pleasure, health, long life, a lusty old age, nay, after death a sitting at the right hand of our Saviour in His kingdom.

Though as to this last part of their happiness they care not how long it be deferred, having scarce any appetite toward a tasting the joys of heaven; till they are surfeited, glutted with, and can no longer relish their enjoyments on earth. By this easy way of purchasing pardons, any notorious highwayman, any plundering soldier, or any bribe-taking judge shall disburse some part of their unjust gains, and so think all their grossest impieties sufficiently atoned for. So many perjuries, lusts, drunkenness, quarrels, bloodsheds, cheats, treacheries, shall all be, as it were, struck a bargain for, and such a contract made, as if they had paid off all arrears and might now begin upon a new score.

And what can be more ridiculous than for some others to be confident of going to heaven by repeating daily those seven verses out of the Psalms, which the devil taught St. Bernard; thinking thereby to have put a trick upon him, but that he was overreached in his cunning.

Several of these fooleries, which are so gross and absurd as I myself am even ashamed to own, are practiced and admired, not only by the vulgar, but by such proficients in religion as one might well expect should have more wit.

From the same principles of folly proceeds the custom of each country's challenging their particular guardian-saint. Nay, each saint has his distinct office alloted to him and is accordingly addressed to upon the respective occasions: one for the toothache, a second to grant an easy delivery in childbirth, a third to help persons to lost goods, another to protect seamen in a long voyage, a fifth to guard the farmer's cows and sheep, and so on. For to rehearse all instances would be extremely tedious.

There are some more catholic saints petitioned to upon all occasions, as more especially the Virgin Mary, whose blind devotees think it manners now to place the mother before the Son.

And of all the prayers and intercessions that are made to these respective saints the substance of them is no more than downright folly. Among all the trophies that for tokens of gratitude are hung upon the walls and ceilings of churches, you shall find no relics presented as a memorandum of any that were ever cured of folly, or had been made one dram the wiser.

One perhaps after shipwreck got safe to shore; another recovered when he had been run through by an enemy; one, when all his fellow-soldiers were killed upon the spot, as cunningly perhaps as cowardly, made his escape from the field; another while he was a-hanging, the rope broke, and so he saved his neck and renewed his license for practicing his old trade of thieving; another broke gaol and got loose; a patient, against his physician's will, recovered of a dangerous fever; another drank poison, which putting him into a violent looseness, did his body more good than hurt, to the great grief of his wife who hoped upon this occasion to have become a joyful widow; another had his wagon overturned, and yet none of his horses lamed; another had . . . a grievous fall, and yet recovered from the bruise; another had been tampering with his neighbor's wife, and escaped very narrowly from being caught by the enraged cuckold in the very act.

After all these acknowledgments of escapes from such singular dangers, there is none, as I have before intimated, that return thanks for being freed from folly, folly being so sweet and luscious that it is rather sued for as happiness than deprecated as a punishment. But why should I launch out into so wide a sea of superstitions?

> Had I as many tongues as Argus eyes,
> Briareus hands, they all would not suffice
> Folly in all her shapes t'epitomize.

Almost all Christians [are] wretchedly enslaved to blindness and ignorance, while the priests, . . . so far from preventing or removing, . . . blacken the darkness and promote the delusion. [They] Wisely foresee that the people, like cows which never give down their milk so well as when they are gently stroked, would part with less if they knew more, their bounty proceeding only from a mistake of charity.

Now if any grave wise man should stand up and unseasonably speak the truth, telling every one that a pious life is the only way of securing a happy death; that the best title to a pardon of our sins is purchased by a hearty abhorence of our guilt and sincere resolutions of amendment; that the best devotion which can be paid to any saints is to imitate them in their exemplary life—if he should proceed thus to inform them of their several mistakes, there would be quite another estimate put upon tears, watchings, masses, fastings, and other severities, which before were so much prized, as persons will now be vexed to lose that satisfaction they formerly found in them. . . .

The next to these are another sort of brainsick fools, who style themselves monks and of religious orders, though they assume both titles very unjustly. For as to the last, they have very little religion in them; and as to the former, the etymology of the word monk implies a solitariness, or being alone; whereas they are so thick abroad that we cannot pass any street or alley without meeting them. Now I cannot imagine . . . [any] degree of men [who] would be more hopelessly wretched, if I did not stand their friend and buoy them up in that lake of misery which by the engagements of a holy vow they have voluntarily immerged themselves in.

But when these sort of men are so unwelcome to others . . . that the very sight of them is thought ominous, I yet make them highly in love with themselves and fond admirers of their own happiness. The first step whereunto they esteem a profound ignorance, thinking carnal knowledge a great enemy to their spiritual welfare, and seem confident of becoming greater proficients in divine mysteries the less they are poisoned with any human learning. They imagine that they bear a sweet consort with the heavenly choir when they tone out their daily tally of psalms, which they rehearse only by rote, without permitting their understanding or affections to go along with their voice.

Among these, some make a good profitable trade of beggary, going about from house to house, not like the apostles, to break, but to beg, their bread. Nay, [they] thrust into all public houses, come aboard the passage-boats, get into the traveling wagons, and omit no opportunity of time or place for the craving people's charity; doing a great deal of injury to common highway beggars by interloping in their traffic of alms. And when they are thus voluntarily poor, destitute, not provided with two coats nor with any money in their purse, they have the impudence to pretend that they imitate the first disciples, whom their Master expressly sent out in such an equipage.

It is pretty to observe how they regulate all their actions as it were by weight and measure to so exact a proportion, as if the whole loss of their religion depended upon the omission of the least punctilio. Thus they must be very critical in the precise number of knots to the tying on of their sandals; what distinct colors their respective habits, and of what stuff made; how broad and long their girdles; how big and in what fashion their hoods, whether their bald crowns be to a hair's breadth of the right cut; how many hours they must sleep, at what minute rise to prayers, etc.

And these several customs are altered according to the humors of different persons and places. While they are sworn to the superstitious observance of these trifles, they do not only despise all others, but are very inclined to fall out among themselves; for though they make profession of an apostolic charity, yet they will pick a quarrel and be implacably passionate for such poor provocations as the girding on a coat the wrong way, [or] the wearing of clothes a little too darkish colored, or any such nicety not worth the speaking of. Some are so obstinately superstitious that they will wear their upper garment of some coarse dog's hair stuff, and that next their skin as soft as silk. But others, on the contrary, will have linen frocks outermost, and their shirts of wool or hair. Some again will not touch a piece of money, though they make no scruple of drunkenness and the lust of the flesh.

All their several orders are mindful of nothing more than of their being distinguished from each other by their different customs and habits. They seem, indeed, not so careful of becoming like Christ and of being known to be his disciples, as the being unlike to one another and distinguishable for followers of their several founders. A great part of their religion consists in their title. Some will be called cordeliers, and these subdivided into capuchines, minors, minims, and mendicants; some again are styled Benedictines, others of the order of St. Bernard, others of that of St. Bridget; some are Augustin monks, some Willielmites, and others Jacobists, as if the common name of Christian were too mean and vulgar.

Most of them place their greatest stress for salvation on a strict conformity to their foppish ceremonies and a belief of their legendary traditions. Wherein they fancy to have acquitted themselves with so much of supererogation, that one heaven can never be a condign reward for their meritorious life; little thinking that the Judge of all the earth at the last day shall put them off, with a "Who hath required these things at your hands?" and call them to account only for the stewardship of His legacy, which was the precept of love and charity.

It will be pretty to hear their pleas before the great tribunal. One will brag how he mortified his carnal appetite by feeding only upon fish. Another will urge that he spent most of his time on earth in the divine exercise of singing psalms. A third will tell how many days he fasted, and what severe penance he imposed on himself for the bringing his body into subjection. Another shall produce in his own behalf as many ceremonies as would load a fleet of merchantmen. A fifth shall plead that in threescore years he never so much as touched a piece of money, except he fingered it through a thick pair of gloves. A sixth, to testify his former humility, shall bring along with him his sacred hood, so old and nasty that any seaman had rather stand bareheaded on the deck than put it on to defend his ears in the sharpest storms. The next that comes to answer for himself shall plead that for fifty years together he had lived like a sponge upon the same place, and was content never to change his homely habitation. Another shall whisper softly and tell the Judge he has lost his voice by a continual singing of holy hymns and anthems. The next shall confess how he fell into a lethargy by a strict, reserved, and sedentary life. And the last shall intimate that he has forgot to speak by having always kept silence, in obedience to the injunction of taking heed lest he should have offended with his tongue.

But amidst all their fine excuses our Saviour shall interrupt them with this answer, "Woe unto you, scribes and pharisees, hypocrites, verily I know you not; I left you but one precept, of loving one another, which I do not hear any one plead he has faithfully discharged; I told you plainly in my gospel, without any parable, that my Father's kingdom was prepared not for such as should lay claim to it by austerities, prayers, or fastings, but for those who should render themselves worthy of it by the exercise of faith and the offices of charity. I cannot own such as depend on their own merits without a reliance on my mercy; as many of you therefore as trust to the broken reeds of your own deserts may even go search out a new heaven, for you shall never enter into that which from the foundations of the world was prepared only for such as are true of heart. . . ."

And now for some reflections upon popes, cardinals and bishops, who in pomp and splendor have almost equalled if not [outdone] secular princes. Now if any one consider that their upper crotchet of white linen is to signify their unspotted purity and innocence; that their forked mitres, with both divisions tied together by the same knot, are to denote the joint knowledge of the Old and New Testament. That their always wearing gloves represents their keeping their hands clean and undefiled from lucre and covetousness; that the pastoral staff implies the care of a flock committed to their charge; that the cross carried before them expresses their victory over all carnal affection. He that considers this, and much more of the like nature, must needs conclude they are entrusted with a very weighty and difficult office. But alas, they think it sufficient if they can but feed themselves; and as to their flock, either commend them to the care of Christ Himself, or commit them to the guidance of some inferior vicars and curates. [They do] Not so much as remember what their name of bishop imports, to wit, labor, pains and diligence, but by base simoniacal contracts, they are in a profane sense *Episcopi*, i.e. overseers of their own gain and income.

So cardinals, in like manner, if they did but consider that the church supposes them to succeed in the room of the apostles; that therefore they must behave themselves as their predecessors, and so not be lords, but dispensers of spiritual gifts, of the disposal whereof they must one day render a strict account. Or if they would but reflect a little on their habit, and thus reason with themselves, what means this white upper garment, but only an unspotted innocence? What signifies my inner purple, but only an ardent love and zeal to God? What imports my outermost pall, so wide and long that it covers the whole mule when I ride, nay, should be big enough to cover a camel, but only a diffusive charity that should spread itself for a succor and protection to all, by teaching, exhorting, comforting, reproving, admonishing, composing of differences, courageously withstanding wicked princes and sacrificing for the safety of our flock our life and blood, as well as our wealth and riches. Though indeed riches ought not to be at all possessed by such as boast themselves successors to the apostles, who were poor, needy and destitute. I say, if they did but lay these considerations to heart they would never be so ambitious of being created to this honor; they would willingly resign it when conferred upon them, or at least would be as industrious, watchful and laborious as the primitive apostles were.

Now as to the popes of Rome, who pretend themselves Christ's vicars, if they would but imitate His exemplary life, . . . an unintermitted course of preaching [and] attendance with poverty, nakedness, hunger and a contempt of this world; if they did but consider the import of the word pope, which signifies a father; or if they did but practice their surname of most holy, what order or degrees of men would be in a worse condition? There would be then no such vigorous making of parties and buying of votes in the conclave upon the vacancy of that see.

And those who, by bribery or other indirect courses, should get themselves elected would never secure their sitting firm in the chair by pistol, poison, force and violence. How much of their pleasure would be abated if they were but endowed with one dram of wisdom? Wisdom, did I say? Nay, with one grain of that salt which our Saviour bid them not lose the savor of. All their riches, all their honor, their jurisdictions, their Peter's patrimony, their offices, their dispensations, their licenses, their indulgences, their long train and attendants, see in how short a compass I have abbreviated all their marketing of religion; in a word, all their perquisites would be forfeited and lost; and in their [place] would succeed watchings, fastings, tears, prayers, sermons, hard studies, repenting sighs and a thousand such like severe penalties. Nay, what's yet more deplorable, it would then follow that all their clerks, amanuenses, notaries, advocates, proctors, secretaries, the offices of grooms, ostlers, serving-men, pimps and somewhat else which for modesty's sake I shall not mention; in short, all these troops of attendants which depend on his holiness would all lose their several employments. This indeed would be hard, but what yet remains would be more dreadful. The very Head of the Church, the spiritual prince, would then be brought from all his splendor to the poor equipage of a scrip and staff.

But all this is upon the supposition only that they understood what circumstances they are placed in; whereas now, by a wholesome neglect of thinking, they live as well as heart can wish. Whatever of toil and drudgery belongs to their office, that they assign over to St. Peter or St. Paul, who have time enough to mind it; but if there be anything of pleasure and grandeur, that they assume to themselves . . . So that by my influence no sort of people live more to their own ease and content. They think to satisfy that Master they pretend to serve, our Lord and Saviour, with their great state and magnificence, with the ceremonies of installments, with the titles of reverence and holiness, and with exercising their episcopal function only in blessing and cursing.

2. Erasmus: The Enchiridion

The Enchiridion, a handbook or dagger of a Christian soldier, is the treatise of Erasmus which illustrates better than any other the nature of the *philosophia Christi* which he promoted. He wrote it, according to his own account, for a hot-tempered and dissolute soldier named John, whose pious wife was concerned about her husband's salvation. Erasmus was a refugee in the castle of Tournehem at the time (1501), where a group of friends fled from the plague raging in Paris. The *Enchiridion* stressed the need for the personal interiorization of piety and the spiritualization of religious practice. Drawing heavily upon the fathers of the ancient church and upon the moral preachings of the classics, Erasmus stressed the need to take up arms against spiritual foes, to use prayer to acquire knowledge of the spiritual meaning of the Scriptures, to imitate Christ. He followed this up with twenty-two rules for leading a godly life and with remedies for special vices. *The Enchiridion* appeared in many Latin editions and was early translated into several vernacular languages, a highly influential writing. From *Advocates of Reform* (volume XIV: The Library of Christian Classics), edited by Matthew Spinka. First published in MCMLIII by the SCM Press Ltd., London and the Westminster Press, Philadelphia. Used by permission of Westminster/John Knox Press.

Erasmus of Rotterdam to John the German His Courtier Friend, Greeting: You have entreated with no ordinary zeal, best beloved brother in the Lord, that I prescribe for you a sort of compendious guide for living, that having been instructed by it, you can arrive at a state of mind worthy of Christ. Indeed you say that while for a long time you have been pushing forward in court life, you have been concerned how you can flee from Egypt with its vices and delights, and with Moses as leader be happily set upon the road to virtue. You are so dear to me that I rejoice exceedingly in our salutary proposal, which I hope (at least with regard to our need). He who has deigned to arouse you to it will make prosper-

23

ous and carry forward. Yet I have with too much willingness
yielded to you as a man and friend, or as one yearning for pious
sentiments. But you strive not to appear to have begged our assistance without cause, else might I seem fruitlessly to have gratified
your wish. Indeed with common prayers let us implore that kindly
spirit of Jesus, that it may suggest to me as I write words which
bear salvation, and render them efficacious for you.

In Life Man Must Be Watchful

First of all, as you too must remember, Job (that vet-
eran, undefeated soldier) testifies that the life of mortals is nothing
else than a sort of perpetual warfare, and that the generality of
mankind is too often deceived, whose minds that schemer, the
world, holds in the grips of the most seductive wantonness. These
folk, as if the war were already brought to an end, celebrate un-
seasonable holidays, when nothing could be so unlike *real* peace.
It is wonderful in how much security they live, and in what a
leisurely manner they go to sleep in both ears, while we are end-
lessly attacked by so many ironclad troops of vices, are laid hold of
by so many artifices, and are fallen upon by so many stratagems.
Behold, in your last going forth they keep watch upon you with
the highest vigilance, these most worthless demons, armed against
us with a thousand deceits, a thousand noxious arts, who strive
with fiery darts and poison arrows to pierce our minds from above;
no javelin of Hercules or Cephalus was ever more certain than
these weapons, unless they be fended off by the impenetrable shield
of faith. Time and again the world attacks us here, from right and
left, from front and rear, the world of which John speaks as entirely constituted in vices, and [which seems] to Christ himself
sometimes unsafe, sometimes unseen. Nor, indeed, is the reason for
attack a simple one. For at one time in adverse circumstances, raging like Mars undisguised, the world shakes the walls of the mind
with a heavy battering ram; at another time, by large but exceedingly vain promises, it incites the mind to betrayal; at still another
time, by secretly contrived pitfalls, unexpectedly it snatches the
mind, so that between the negligent and the secure it oppresses us
all. Finally, that slimy snake, first betrayer of our peace, now

hidden by its green hue in the grass, now concealing its hundred coils in dark grottoes, desists not from lying in wait for the heels of our woman once she has been corrupted. Understand "woman" as the carnal part of man. For this is our Eve, through whom the most crafty serpent lures our mind to death-bearing pleasures. As if it were not enough for him so to threaten at the door, we at last bear the enemy within the inner recesses of our mind, more than we would a close friend, more than a servant. . . . Here, indeed, is that old earthly Adam, in habit more than a citizen, in zeal more than an enemy, whom it is not permitted to enclose with an entrenchment, nor possible to drive out with an army. Him we ought to watch with a hundred eyes, lest perchance he may lay open God's fortress to demons.

Therefore since all of us are engaged in such a formidable and difficult war, and with such numerous enemies so sworn and devoted to our destruction, so watchful, so armed, so treacherous, so experienced, are we not insane not to take up arms against them, not to stand our watch, not to hold all things suspect? Accordingly, then, just as in quite peaceful times, we snore stretched out, we leave off work, we indulge in pleasure, and (as they say) at leisure take care of our own little skin. One would think that our life were a Greek drinking bout, not a war, so do we wrap ourselves in bedclothes rather than armor and skins, we are girded with the rosy delights of Adonis rather than with hard arms, we indulge ourselves with luxury and ease in place of military efforts, we practice upon the peaceful harp rather than the javelins of Mars. As if not this sort of peace, but war, were the most loathsome of all things!

Indeed he who enters into peace with vices violates the agreement struck with God in baptism. And you insanely cry, "Peace, peace," when you hold God as an enemy, who alone is peace and the author of peace! And clearly He proclaims through the mouth of the prophet, saying, "There is no peace to the wicked." Nor is there any other condition of peace with Him, unless, while we fight in the garrison of the body with great hatred and the highest force, we wage war upon vices. Otherwise, if we consort with them, we shall doubly make our foe Him who alone can as a friend bless us, as an enemy damn us. First, we stand by those vices with which God can in no wise agree (for what has light to do with darkness?) Second, we, most ungrateful, do not stand by our pledge to Him, and with the most sacred ceremonies we impiously fend off the fell blow. Or perhaps you do not know, O Christian soldier, when you were already being initiated into the mysteries of the life-giving bath, that you gave yourself by name to Christ as your leader, to whom you doubly owed life, at one and the same time given and restored, and hence you owe more to Him than to yourself? If you should too little stand by your covenant, does it not occur to you that you pledged yourself to such a kindly leader, that you dedicated your head, bound by His sacraments as if by a votive offering, to His fateful purposes?

To what purpose was He delaying to impress the sign of the cross on your brow, unless, while yet alive, you might fight under His banner? To what end was He putting off anointing you with His sacred ointment, unless that you might undertake an eternal struggle with vices? What great shame, what almost public execration of humankind, for a man to cut himself off from his princely leader! Why do you hold Christ your leader in derision, neither compelled by fear of Him, since He is God, nor forbidden by love of Him, since for your sake He is man? Bearing His word before you, you ought to have been warned what you promised to Him. Why treacherously do you desert to the enemy, when once He redeemed you by the price of His blood? Why as a double deserter do you serve in the army of the enemy? With what impudence do you dare to raise the hostile battle standards against your King (who expended His life for your sake)? For he who does not stand for Him, as He has said, stands against Him, and he who does not gather with Him, He scatters.

Moreover, you deserve not only a loathsome title but also a most wretched pay. You wish to hear what your pay is, whoever you are who fight for the world? Paul, that standard-bearer of the Christian warfare, replied, "The wages of sin is death." Who, then, would undertake this splendid warfare, if the death of the body were proposed to him? Will you indeed bear such a loathsome death of the soul, obtaining it in place of a reward? In these insane wars, which men wage with men either in beastly madness or out of miserable necessity, do you not see, if at any time either the magnitude of promised booty or the dreaded cruelty of the victor, or the disgrace of reproached cowardice, or, finally, the desire for praise, has goaded the minds of the soldiers; by what eager effort they accomplish whatever toil there is, what an empty life they lead, with how great ardor they are taken prisoner into the enemy camp? And what a paltry pay, I ask you, is sought with so much attention, so much zeal, by these miserable folk? Surely it is that by this mere human leader they may be honored with the noisy ovation of soldiers and camp and with elegant little odes, that they may be wreathed about with a grassy crown or with oaken leaves, that they may bring home a little more pay. We, on the contrary, are aroused neither by shame nor by reward, since we now have the same One as spectator of our struggle as we are one day going to have as Giver of our reward. What rewards has our Agonothetes proposed for the victor? Surely not mules, such as Homer pictures Achilles as receiving, or tripods Virgil Aeneas, but that which "neither eye has seen, nor ear heard, nor has ascended into the heart of man," and this indeed imparts meanwhile a sort of solace of labors for those who are still struggling. What then? Happy immortality. But in those absurd struggles glory is the chief part of the prize, and the resources of the conquered are distributed by lot. As far as we are concerned, the affair is carried on under a great and double danger, nor is the struggle concerned with praise, but rather with the head. And as the highest pay proposed ought to go to him who has stuck to his task, so the highest punishment ought to be meted out to him who deserts it. Heaven is promised to him who fights strenuously, and does not the widowed virtue of a generous mind glow with the hope of such a happy prize? Especially if it is promised by that Author who can no more deceive than be unable to be. . . .

It is the body's nature to perish, because even if no one kills it it cannot remain alive. But for the soul to die is a matter of extreme misfortune. With what caution do we remove the wounds of our mere body; with what solicitude do we doctor them? And yet we neglect the wounds of the soul? How we hold in horror the frightful death of the body, because it is seen with bodily eyes! To be sure, since no one sees the soul dying, few believe and very few are frightened, although this death is as much more awful than that one as the soul is greater than the body, as God is greater than the soul.

Do you wish for yourself signs, such as I might point out, by which you may discover either disease or death of the soul? The stomach has indigestion; it cannot retain food. From this you recognize a disease of the body. Bread is not as much the food of the body as the Word of God is the food of the soul. If it is bitter to you, if it tastes nauseous, what doubt is there that the palate of your soul is infected with disease? If it does not retain victuals, if it does not pass them into your intestines, you evidently have proof that your soul is sick. When your knees totter and your sick limbs can scarcely be dragged about, do you not recognize that you have a bad body? And have you not contracted a disease of the mind when it languishes, is nauseated toward all duties of piety, when strength does not suffice for bearing light abuse, when by the expenditure of a mere pittance it is broken? After the sight leaves the eyes, when the ears fail to hear, and after the whole body has been overwhelmed, no one doubts that the soul has departed. When you have the eyes of the heart obscured so that you do not see the brightest light (that is, truth), when you do not perceive with your inner ears the divine voice, when you lack every sense, do you believe the soul to be alive? You see your brother suffering indignities, yet your mind is not in the least moved. . . . Why at this point does your soul feel nothing? Surely because it is dead. Wherefore dead? Because God, its life, is not present. Where God is, there is love. For "God is love." Otherwise if you are a living member, why is any part of your body in pain when you are not only not in pain, but also not feeling anything? Here is another sign which is even more certain. You have defrauded a friend, you have committed adultery, your soul has received a major wound, and yet up to now it is not in pain, so that you . . . rejoice over gain and boast that you have committed wickedness. Surely you must consider that your soul lies dead. . . .

On the other hand, in the words of the Gospel the disciples say to Christ: "O Lord, whither shall we go? You have the words of life." Why "words of life"? Surely because they flowed forth from that Soul from which never even for a moment did divinity depart, which likewise restores us to everlasting life. But when Paul was ill in body, the Physician took care of him. Not rarely have pious men recalled a lifeless body to life. But God does not revive a dead soul except by a singular and gratuitous power, and certainly does not resuscitate it if dead it leaves the body. Then the sense of bodily death is either nothing or at least certainly very brief, while the sense of the soul's death is everlasting. And besides, the soul is more than dead, yet, in some fashion or other, to the sense of death it is somehow immortal. Then since we ought to struggle against such a new danger, what is that stupor, that false sense of security, that supineness in our minds, which not even the fear of a very great misfortune rouses up?

Yet, on the contrary, it is nothing for either greatness of danger or the enemies' resources, power and artifices to perplex your mind. He helps him whom you hold to be a serious adversary; He will straightway help him whom you hold as your present succorer. There are innumerable ones against you, but He who stands for you is One more able to stand for all. "If God is for us, who is against us?" If He sustains us, what is lacking? Take upon yourself the vow of victory with your whole heart. Your encounter is not with an unbroken enemy, but with One already once broken, melted, stripped, yet till now triumphant over us. Think upon Christ our Head, by whom the devil will without doubt in turn be conquered. Think also upon ourselves. Take care that you are in the Body, and you will be able to do all things in the Head. In yourself you are indeed exceedingly foolish; in Him you avail something.

Hence, therefore, the outcome of our Mars is not at all doubtful, for the reason that victory in no wise depends upon fortune, but all this lies in the hand of God, and, through Him, also in our hands. Here no one has failed to conquer unless He did not want to conquer. The Helper's kindness has never been lacking to anyone; if you took care not to lack His kindness, you were victorious. He will fight for you, and will impute His liberality to you for merit. You must understand every victory as received of Him, who, first and alone immune from sin, oppressed the tyranny of sin, yet bestows these blessings upon you not without your own effort. For He who said, "Trust in me, for I have conquered the world," wishes you to be of a great, not a secure, mind. Thus at last we will conquer through Him, if we fight according to His example. Wherefore we ought to steer a middle course between Scylla and Charybdis, so that we neither act too securely because we rely on Divine Grace nor cast away our mind with our arms because we are dispirited by the difficulties of war.

Of the Weapons of the Christian Warfare

I think that principle which among the first pertains to the discipline of this military service is that you give especial thought and consideration to what kind of arms is most powerful for the sort of enemies you must encounter; then that you have them always in readiness lest at any time that wiliest of schemers may crush you unarmed and unaware. In your earthly wars it is quite common for you to pause either while the enemy is in winter quarters or when there is a period of truce. For us while as yet we fight in this body it is not permitted to be separated even a finger's breadth (as they say) from our arms. Never should we fail to stand in the battle line, never should we cease to keep watch, because our enemy never ceases in his attacks. Verily, when he is peaceful, when he pretends flight or a truce, then he is most of all preparing traps; nor ought we ever more cautiously to stand watch than when he shows the appearance of peace; never ought we to be less frightened by him than when he rises against us in open war. Therefore let the first care be that the mind be not unarmed. . . .

. . . Two weapons should especially be prepared for him who must fight those seven nations—the Canaanites, the Hittites, the Amorites, the Perizzites, the Girgashites, the Hivites, the Jebusites; that is— . . . the whole troop of vices, of which the seven capital sins are numbered most powerful. These two weapons are prayer and knowledge. Paul always expresses the desire that men be so armed, for he commands them to pray without ceasing. Pure prayer directed to heaven subdues passion, for it is a citadel inaccessible to the enemy. Knowledge furnishes the intellect with salutary opinions so that nothing else may be lacking.

> "So truly does each claim the other's aid,
> and make with it a friendly league."

The former implores, but the latter suggests what should be prayed for, that you should pray eagerly, and, according to James, "nothing wavering." Faith and hope prove that you should seek the things of salvation in Jesus' name; knowledge shows you how to do this. The sons of Zebedee heard from Christ these words: "You do not know what you seek." But prayer is indeed more powerful, making it possible to converse with God; yet knowledge is no less necessary. . . .

But hear what Christ teaches us in Matthew's Gospel: "When you pray, do not talk much as the heathen do, for they think they shall be heard for their much speaking. Be not therefore like them, for your Father knows what your need is before you ask him." And Paul contemns ten thousand words spoken in the spirit, that is, with the lips, in favor of five put forth in the understanding. . . . Then, therefore, you should familiarize yourself with this fact: when the enemy attacks and the remaining vices molest you, you should immediately with sure faith arouse your mind toward heaven, whence comes your help. But also raise your hands to heaven. It is safest to be occupied with the duties of piety, that your works may be concerned, not with earthly studies, but with Christ.

But lest you contemn the support of knowledge, consider this. . . . Believe me, dearest beloved brother, there is no attack of the enemy so violent, that is, no temptation so formidable, that an eager study of the Scriptures will not easily beat it off; there is no adversity so sad that it does not render it bearable. . . . For all Holy Scripture was divinely inspired and perfected by God its Author. What is small is the lowliness of the Word, hiding under almost sordid words the greatest mysteries. What is dazzling is no doctrine of mortals, for it is not blemished by any blot of error; the doctrine of Christ alone is wholly snow-white, wholly dazzling, wholly pure. What is inflexible and rough expresses the mystery clothed in the letter. If anyone touches the surface, the pod, what is harder and harsher? They did not taste the manna without the husk who spoke, "That is a hard saying, and who can hear it?" Pluck out the spiritual sense; now nothing is sweeter, nothing more succulent. The word *manna* sounds to the Hebrews like "What is this?" This agrees beautifully [with] divine Scripture, which contains nothing idle, nor one tittle . . . not worthy of these words, "What is this?" . . . For what is the water concealed in the veins of the earth but the mystical meaning imprisoned in the letter? What is this same water when it is made to gush forth but the mystical meaning drawn out and explained? Because it is spread far and wide for the edification of the hearers, what prevents its being called a river?

Therefore if you will dedicate yourself wholly to the study of the Scriptures, if you will meditate on the law of the Lord day and night, you will not be afraid of the terror of the night or of the day, but you will be fortified and trained against every onslaught of enemies. Nor would I, for my part, disapprove your taking your preliminary training for military service in the writings of the pagan poets and philosophers, but gradually, at the proper age, . . . and cursorily—not tarrying, as it were, to perish on the sirens' rocks. Saint Basil also calls the young to these studies to establish them in Christian morals and recall them to the muses. Our Augustine was his pupil. Nor is Jerome displeased by the well-beloved captive. Cyprian is praised because he adorned the temple of the Lord with the spoils of Egypt, but I do not want you to imbibe the morals of the Gentiles along with their letters. And yet you will find out very many things there conductive to right living. Nor ought you to despise pagan authors, for they too are often good moral teachers. Moses did not despise the advice of his father-in-law, Jethro. Those letters shape and nourish the child's nature and wonderfully prepare one for the understanding of divine Scriptures, to break in upon which with unwashed feet and hands is almost a sacrilege. Jerome belabors the impudence of those who, advanced in secular studies, dare to treat the divine Scriptures, yet how much more shamelessly do they act who not even having tasted Scripture dare so to do!

But as divine Scripture does not bear much fruit if you persist in and cling to the letter, so is the poetry of Homer or Virgil quite useful if you remember the whole of it to be allegorical. That is something no one will deny who finds the learning of the ancients supremely to his taste. I will not at all insist that you undertake the study of obscene poets—certainly not to look into them more deeply—unless perhaps you learn rather to abhor the vices described and by the contention of wicked things more strongly to love honest ones. Among the philosophers I would prefer you to follow the Platonists, for . . . in very many of their opinions and in their way of speaking they approach as closely as possible the prophetic and Gospel pattern. . . . Therefore as soon as you feel nausea, you ought to hasten as fast as possible to the manna of heavenly wisdom, which will abundantly nourish and revive you, until as victor you reach those palms of promised reward which will never be lacking. . . .

But as you so desire (lest we seem not to have complied with your wishes) an *enchiridion*, a dagger which we are to forge, [here is] one that you are never to lay down from your hand, even when you are eating or sleeping. Even if you are forced to travel in the business of this world and become wearied at bearing around this righteous armor, yet you should not leave yourself even for a moment totally unarmed, lest that wily foe should oppress you. Be not ashamed, then, to have this little sword with you, neither a burden to carry nor useless for defending yourself. It is indeed very small, but skillfully use it, together with the shield of faith, and you will easily sustain the enemy's tumultuous assault and avert a deadly wound. But now is the time for us to teach ourselves a sort of "manual of arms." And I promise you, if you exercise yourself diligently in it, our sovereign Christ will transfer you, rejoicing and victorious, from this garrison to the city of Jerusalem, where there is no tumult of war at all, but everlasting peace and perfect tranquillity. Meanwhile all hope of safety rests in iron.

3. Hutten: Letter to Elector Frederick of Saxony

Ulrich von Hutten, a German knight and young humanist, was one of the most articulate spokesmen for a kind of German cultural nationalism. He carried on a vendetta against ecclesiastical abuses, the monastic orders, scholastic barbarism, and the exploitation of the Germans by the Roman church. "He is," wrote a fellow humanist Mutian, "sharp and vehement and a great poet, but such that he can be irritated by the slightest word!" Hutten extended his literary attacks against the prelates and popes such as Julius II and Leo X. With tension mounting he feared for life and sought refuge in Ebernburg, the castle of the imperial knight Franz von Sickingen. From there on September 11, 1520, he wrote the following letter to Luther's protector, Elector Frederick of Saxony. From Merrick Whitcomb, *A Literary Source-Book of the German Renaissance* (Philadelphia: University of Pennsylvania, 1899), II, 6, 19-20.

We see that there is no gold and almost no silver in our German land. What little may perhaps be left is drawn away daily by the new schemes invented by the council of the most holy members of the Roman Curia. What is thus squeezed out of us is put to the most shameful uses. Would you know, dear Germans, what employment I have myself seen that they make at Rome of our money? It does not lie idle! Leo X gives a part to nephews and relatives (these are so numerous that there is a proverb at Rome, "As thick as Leo's relations"). A portion is consumed by so many most reverend cardinals (of which the holy father created no less than one and thirty in a single day), as well as to support innumerable referendaries, auditors, prothonotaries, abbreviators, apostolic secretaries, chamberlains and a variety of officials forming the elite of the great head Church. These in turn draw after them at untold expense, copyists, beadles, messengers, servants, scullions, mule drivers, grooms, and an innumerable army of prostitutes and of the most degraded followers. They maintain dogs, horses, monkeys, long-tailed apes and many more such creatures for their pleasure. They construct houses all of marble. They have precious stones, are clothed in purple and fine linen and dine sumptuously, frivolously indulging themselves in every species of luxury. In short, a vast number of the worst of men are supported in Rome in idle indulgence by means of our money. . . . Does not Your Grace perceive how many bold robbers, how many cunning hypocrites commit repeatedly the greatest crimes under the monk's cowl, and how many crafty hawks feign the simplicity of doves, and how many ravening wolves simulate the innocence of lambs? And although there be a few truly pious among them, even they cling to superstition and pervert the law of life which Christ laid down for us.

Now, if all these who devastate Germany and continue to devour everything might once be driven out, and an end made of their unbridled plundering, swindling and deception, with which the Romans have overwhelmed us, we should again have gold and silver in sufficient quantities and should be able to keep it. And then this money, in such supply and value as it may be present, might be put to better uses, for example: . . . [that] great armaments . . . [may be raised to] extend the boundaries of the empire; also that the Turks may be conquered, if this seems desirable; that many who, because of poverty, steal and rob may honestly earn their living once more, and that those who otherwise must starve may receive from the state contributions to mitigate their need; that scholars may be helped and the study of the arts and sciences and of good literature advanced; above all that every virtue may receive its reward; want be relieved at home; indolence banished and deceit killed.

Then, too, the Bohemians, when they come to know this, will make common cause with us, for it was material obstacles alone that kept them back, in earlier times, from dealing with the avarice of their priests. The Greeks would do the same, who, unable to bear the Romish tyranny, have been for a long time, at the instigation of the popes, regarded as heretics. The Russians would also become Christians and join us, they who, when recently they proposed to embrace Christianity, were repelled by the demand of His Holiness for a yearly tribute of 400,000 ducats to be levied upon them. Even the Turks would thereby hate us less; and no heathen, as formerly, would have occasion to molest us. For up to the present day the shameful lives of the heads of the church have made the name of Christian hateful to all strangers.

Part Two

LUTHER'S EVANGELICAL BREAKTHROUGH

1. Luther: Preface to the Epistle of St. Paul to the Romans

On October 19, 1512, Martin Luther became a doctor of theology in the University of Wittenberg, a promotion which made it possible for him to assume the chair of Biblical theology. He lectured on the Psalms and then in 1515-1516 on St. Paul's *Epistle to the Romans*. His brilliant commentary on Romans, a work of genius growing from the depths of great scholarship and intense spiritual struggle, revealed his evangelical insight that man is justified by God's grace alone through faith in Christ. During the years which followed he clarified his thought further, and shortly before the publication of his translation of the New Testament in German in 1522 he wrote the following *Preface to Romans* which defines clearly his understanding of the relationship of God's law and the gospel, a religious breakthrough of momentous historical consequences. From Bertram Lee Woolf, ed., *Reformation Writings of Martin Luther, II* (New York: Philosophical Library, 1956), pp. 284-290. Reprinted by permission of the publishers.

This epistle is in truth the most important document in the New Testament, the gospel in its purest expression. Not only is it well worth a Christian's while to know it word for word by

heart, but also to meditate on it day by day. It is the soul's daily
bread, and can never be read too often or studied too much. The
more you probe into it the more precious it becomes, and the better its flavor. God helping me, I shall try my best to make this
Preface serve as an introduction which will enable everyone to
understand it in the best possible way. Hitherto, this epistle has
been smothered with comments and all sorts of irrelevancies; yet,
in essence, it is a brilliant light, almost enough to illumine the
whole Bible.

The first thing needed is to master the terminology. We must
learn what St. Paul means by such words as law, sin, grace, faith,
righteousness, flesh, spirit, and the like; otherwise we shall read
and only waste our time. You must not understand the term LAW
in its everyday sense as something which explains what acts are
permitted or forbidden. This holds for ordinary laws, and you
keep them by doing what they enjoin, although you may have no
heart in it. But God judges according to your inmost convictions;
His law must be fulfilled in your very heart, and cannot be obeyed
if you merely perform certain acts. Its penalties do indeed apply
to certain acts done apart from our inmost convictions, such as
hypocrisy and lying. Psalm 117 declares that all men are liars, because no one keeps God's law from his heart; nor can he do so, for
to be averse to goodness and prone to evil are traits found in all
men. If we do not choose goodness freely, we do not keep God's
law from the heart. Then sin enters in, and divine wrath is in-
curred even though, to outward appearance, we are doing many
virtuous works and living an honorable life.

In Chapter 2, St. Paul therefore asserts that the Jews are all
sinners. He says that only those who keep the law are righteous in
God's eyes, his point being that no one keeps the law by "works."
Rather, Paul says to the Jews, "You teach us not to commit adultery, but you commit adultery yourselves, since you do the very
things which you condemn." It is as if he were to say, To outward
appearance, you observe the law scrupulously, condemning those
who do not observe it, and being quick to teach one and all. You
see the splinter in the other man's eye, but are unaware of the
timber in your own. Granted that, in appearance and conduct, you
observe the law, owing to your fear of punishment or hope of reward, yet you do nothing from free choice and out of love for the
law, but unwillingly and under compulsion; were there no law,

you would rather do something else. The logical conclusion is that, in the depths of your heart, you hate the law. What is the use of teaching others not to steal if you are a thief at heart yourself and, if you dared, would be one in fact? Of course, the outer conduct of this kind is not continued for long by humbugs of this kind. It follows that, if you teach others but not your own selves, you do not know what you teach and have not rightly understood the nature of the law. Nay, the law increases your guilt, as Paul says in Chapter 5. A man only hates the law the more, the more it demands what he cannot perform.

That is why, in Chapter 7, Paul calls the law spiritual; spiritual because, if the law were corporeal, our works would meet its demands. Since it is spiritual, however, no one keeps it, unless everything you do springs from your inmost heart. Such a heart is given us only by God's spirit, and this spirit makes us equal to the demands of the law. Thus we gain a genuine desire for the law, and then everything is done with willing hearts, and not in fear or under compulsion. Therefore, because that law is spiritual when it is loved by hearts that are spiritual, and demands that sort of mind, if that spirit is not in our hearts, sin remains; a grudge abides together with hostility to the law, although the law itself is right and good and holy.

Therefore, familiarize yourself with the idea that it is one thing to do what the law enjoins and quite another to fulfill the law. All that a man does or ever can do of his own free will and strength is to perform the works required by the law. Nevertheless, all such works are vain and useless as long as we dislike the law and feel it a constraint. That is Paul's meaning in Chapter 3 when he says, "Through the works of the law shall no man be justified before God." It is obvious—is it not?—that the sophisticators wrangling in the schools are misleading when they teach us to prepare ourselves for grace by our works. How can anyone use works to prepare himself to be good when he never does a good work without a certain reluctance or unwillingness in his heart? How is it possible for God to take pleasure in works that spring from reluctant and hostile hearts?

To fulfill the law, we must meet its requirements gladly and lovingly; live virtuous and upright lives without the constraint of the law, and as if neither the law nor its penalties existed. But this joy, this unconstrained love, is put into our hearts by the Holy

Spirit, as St. Paul says in Chapter 5. But the Holy Spirit is given only in, with, and through faith in Jesus Christ, as Paul said in his opening paragraph. Similarly, faith itself comes only through the word of God, the gospel. This gospel proclaims Christ as the Son of God; that He was man; that He died and rose again for our sakes, as Paul says in Chapters 3, 4, and 10.

We reach the conclusion that faith alone justifies us and fulfills the law; and this because faith brings us the spirit gained by the merits of Christ. The spirit, in turn, gives us the happiness and freedom at which the law aims, and this shows that good works really proceed from faith. That is Paul's meaning in Chapter 3 when, after having condemned the works of the law, he sounds as if he had meant to abrogate the law by faith; but says that, on the contrary, we confirm the law through faith, i.e. we fulfill it by faith.

The word SIN in the Bible means something more than the external works done by our bodily action. It means all the circumstances that act together and excite or incite us to do what is done; in particular, the impulses operating in the depths of our hearts. This, again, means that the single term, "doing," includes the case where a man gives way completely and falls into sin. Even where nothing is done outwardly, a man may still fall into complete destruction of body and soul. In particular, the Bible penetrates into our hearts and looks at the root and the very source of all sin, i.e., unbelief in the depth of our heart. Just as faith alone gives us the spirit and the desire for doing works that are plainly good, so unbelief is the sole cause of sin; it exalts the flesh, and gives the desire to do works that are plainly wrong, as happened in the case of Adam and Eve in the garden of Eden, Genesis 3.

Christ therefore singled out unbelief and called it sin. In John 16, He says, The spirit will convict the world of sin because they do not believe in me. Similarly, before good or evil works are performed, and before they appear as good or evil fruits, either faith or unbelief must be already in our hearts. Here are the roots, the sap and the chief energy of all sin. This is what the Bible calls the head of the serpent and of the old dragon, which Christ, the seed of the woman, must crush, as was promised to Adam.

The words GRACE and GIFT differ inasmuch as the true meaning of grace is the kindness of favor which God bears toward us of His own choice, and through which He is willing to give us

Christ, and to pour the Holy Spirit and His blessings upon us. Paul makes this clear in Chapter 5 when he speaks of the grace and favor of Christ, and the like. Nevertheless, both the gifts and the spirit must be received by us daily, although even then they will be incomplete, for the old desires and sins still linger in us and strive against the spirit, as Paul says in Romans 7 and Galatians 5. Again, Genesis 3 speaks of the enmity between the woman's children and the serpent's brood. Yet grace is sufficient to enable us to be accounted entirely and completely righteous in God's sight, because His grace does not come in portions and pieces, separately, like so many gifts; rather, it takes us up completely into its embrace for the sake of Christ our mediator and intercessor, and in order that the gifts may take root in us.

This point of view will help you to understand Chapter 7, where Paul depicts himself as still a sinner; and yet, in Chapter 8, [he] declares that no charge is held against those who are "in Christ," because of the spirit and the (still incomplete) gifts. Insofar as our flesh is not yet killed, we are still sinners. Nevertheless insofar as we believe in Christ, and begin to receive the spirit, God shows us favor and goodwill. He does this to the extent that He pays no regard to our remaining sins and does not judge them; rather He deals with us according to the faith which we have in Christ until sin is killed.

FAITH is not something dreamed, a human illusion, although this is what many people understand by the term. Whenever they see that it is not followed either by an improvement in morals or by good works, while much is still being said about faith, they fall into the error of declaring that faith is not enough, that we must do "works" if we are to become upright and attain salvation. The reason is that, when they hear the gospel, they miss the point; in their hearts, and out of their own resources, they conjure up an idea which they call "belief," which they treat as genuine faith. All the same, it is but a human fabrication, an idea without a corresponding experience in the depths of the heart. It is therefore ineffective and not followed by a better kind of life.

Faith, however, is something that God effects in us. It changes us and we are reborn from God (John 1). Faith puts the old Adam to death and makes us quite different men in heart, in mind and in all our powers; and it is accompanied by the Holy Spirit. O, when it comes to faith, what a living, creative, active, powerful thing it is. It cannot do other than good at all times. It never waits to ask whether there is some good work to do. Rather, before the question is raised, it has done the deed and keeps on doing it. A man not active in this way is a man without faith. He is groping about for faith and searching for good works, but knows neither what faith is nor what good works are. Nevertheless, he keeps on talking nonsense about faith and good works.

Faith is a living and unshakeable confidence, a belief in the grace of God so assured that a man would die a thousand deaths for its sake. This kind of confidence in God's grace, this sort of knowledge of it, makes us joyful, high-spirited and eager in our relations with God and with all mankind. That is what the Holy Spirit effects through faith. Hence the man of faith, without being driven, willingly and gladly seeks to do good to everyone, serve everyone, suffer all kinds of hardships, for the sake of the love and glory of the God who has shown him such grace. It is impossible, indeed, to separate works from faith, just as it is impossible to separate heat and light from fire. Beware, therefore, of wrong conceptions of your own, and of those who talk nonsense while thinking they are pronouncing shrewd judgments on faith and works whereas they are showing themselves the greatest of fools. Offer up your prayers to God, and ask Him to create faith in you; otherwise you will always lack faith, no matter how you try to deceive yourself, or what your efforts and ability.

RIGHTEOUSNESS means precisely the kind of faith we have in mind, and should properly be called "divine righteousness," the righteousness which holds good in God's sight, because it is God's gift and shapes a man's nature to do his duty to all. By his faith, he is set free from sin, and he finds delight in God's commandments. In this way, he pays God the honor that is due to Him, and renders Him what he owes. He serves his fellows willingly according to his ability, so discharging his obligations to all men. Righteousness of this kind cannot be brought about in the ordinary course of nature, by our own free will or by our own powers. No one can give faith to himself, nor free himself from unbelief; how, then, can anyone do away with even his smallest sins? It follows that what is done in the absence of faith on the one hand, or in consequence of unbelief on the other, is naught but falsity, self-deception and sin (Romans 14), no matter how well it is gilded over.

FLESH and SPIRIT must not be understood as if flesh had only to do with moral impurity and spirit only with the state of our hearts. Rather, flesh, according to St. Paul, as also according to Christ in John 3, means everything that is born from the flesh, i.e. the entire self, body and soul, including our reason and all our senses. This is because everything in us leans to the flesh. It is therefore appropriate to call a man "carnal" when, not having yet received grace, he gibbers and jabbers cheerfully about the high things of the spirit in the very way which Galatians 5 depicts as the works of the flesh, and calls hypocrisy and hatred works of the flesh. Moreover, Romans 8 says that the law is weakened by the flesh. This is not said simply of moral impurity, but of all sins. In particular, it is said of lack of faith, which is a kind of wickedness more spiritual in character than anything else.

On the other hand, the term spiritual is often applied to one who is busied with the most outward of works, as when Christ washed His disciples' feet, and when Peter went sailing his boat and fishing. Hence the term "flesh" applies to a person who, in thought and in fact, lives and labors in the service of the body and the temporal life. The term "spirit" applies to a person who, in thought and fact, lives and labors in the service of the spirit and of the life to come. Unless you give these terms this connotation, you will never comprehend Paul's epistle to the Romans, nor any other book of Holy Scripture. Beware then of all teachers who use these terms differently, no matter who they may be, whether Jerome, Augustine, Ambrose, Origen, or their like; or even persons more eminent than they.

2. Luther: Ninety-five Theses
or Disputation on the Power
and Efficacy of Indulgences

Luther's evangelical emphasis upon the full and complete forgiveness of man's sin and his reconciliation with God through God's grace alone led him to question the ecclesiastical practice of selling indulgences. The indulgence or permission to relax the satisfaction to be made by a contrite sinner, even to the point of reducing the suffering of departed souls in purgatory, was a medieval development connected with the history of the sacrament of penance. Luther observed the bad effects of the abusive sale of indulgences, seemingly for money, upon members of his own congregation, when John Tetzel, a Dominican indulgence hawker, came close to the border of Electoral Saxony. Tetzel had been commissioned by Albrecht of Hohenzollern, Archbishop of Mainz, for the sale of a Jubilee indulgence designed to help pay for the new basilica of St. Peter in Rome and to finance Albrecht's debts to the Fugger bankers. Luther prepared the *Theses* for an academic debate on indulgences and according to tradition posted them on the door of the Castle Church in Wittenberg on October 31, 1517. Within a few weeks they were carried to all parts of Christendom and unleashed a storm of controversy that never abated. Reprinted from *Luther's Works*, XXXI, pp. 25-33. Copyright © 1957 Fortress Press. Used by permission of Oxford Fortress Publishers.

Out of love and zeal for truth and the desire to bring it to light, the following theses will be publicly discussed at Wittenberg under the chairmanship of the reverend father Martin Luther, Master of Arts and Sacred Theology and regularly appointed Lecturer on these subjects at that place. He requests that those who cannot be present to debate orally with us will do so by letter.

In the name of Our Lord Jesus Christ. Amen.

1. When our Lord and Master Jesus Christ said, "Repent" [Matt. 4:17], he willed the entire life of believers to be one of repentance.

2. This word cannot be understood as referring to the sacrament of penance, that is, confession and satisfaction as administered by the clergy.

3. Yet it does not mean solely inner repentance; such inner repentance is worthless unless it produces various outward mortifications of the flesh.

4. The penalty of sin remains as long as the hatred of self, that is, true inner repentance, until our entrance into the kingdom of heaven.

5. The pope neither desires nor is able to remit any penalties except those imposed by his own authority or that of the canons.

6. The pope cannot remit any guilt except by declaring and showing that it has been remitted by God; or, to be sure, by remitting guilt in cases reserved to his judgment. If his right to grant remission in these cases were disregarded, the guilt would certainly remain unforgiven.

7. God remits guilt to no one unless at the same time he humbles him in all things and makes him submissive to his vicar, the priest.

8. The penitential canons are imposed only on the living, and, according to the canons themselves, nothing should be imposed on the dying.

9. Therefore the Holy Spirit through the pope is kind to us insofar as the pope in his decrees always makes exception of the article of death and of necessity.

10. Those priests act ignorantly and wickedly who, in the case of the dying, reserve canonical penalties for purgatory.

11. Those tares of changing the canonical penalty to the penalty of purgatory were evidently sown while the bishops slept [Matt. 13:25].

12. In former times canonical penalties were imposed not after but before absolution, as tests of true contrition.

13. The dying are freed by death from all penalties, are already dead as far as the canon laws are concerned, and have a right to be released from them.

14. Imperfect piety or love on the part of the dying person necessarily brings with it great fear; and the smaller the love, the greater the fear.

15. This fear or horror is sufficient in itself, to say nothing of other things, to constitute the penalty of purgatory, since it is very near the horror of despair.

16. Hell, purgatory, and heaven seem to differ the same as despair, fear, and assurance of salvation.

17. It seems as though for the souls in purgatory fear should necessarily decrease and love increase.

18. Furthermore, it does not seem proved, either by reason or Scripture, that souls in purgatory are outside the state of merit, that is, unable to grow in love.

19. Nor does it seem proved that souls in purgatory, at least not all of them, are certain and assured of their own salvation, even if we ourselves may be entirely certain of it.

20. Therefore the pope, when he uses the words "plenary remission of all penalties," does not actually mean "all penalties," but only those imposed by himself.

21. Thus those indulgence preachers are in error who say that a man is absolved from every penalty and saved by papal indulgences.

22. As a matter of fact, the pope remits to souls in purgatory no penalty which, according to canon law, they should have paid in this life.

23. If remission of all penalties whatsoever could be granted to anyone at all, certainly it would be granted only to the most perfect, that is, to very few.

24. For this reason most people are necessarily deceived by that indiscriminate and high-sounding promise of release from penalty.

25. That power which the pope has in general over purgatory corresponds to the power which any bishop or curate has in a particular way in his own diocese or parish.

26. The pope does very well when he grants remission to souls in purgatory, not by the power of the keys, which he does not have, but by way of intercession for them.

27. They preach only human doctrines who say that as soon as the money clinks into the money chest, the soul flies out of purgatory.

28. It is certain that when money clinks in the money chest, greed and avarice can be increased; but when the church intercedes, the result is in the hands of God alone.

29. Who knows whether all souls in purgatory wish to be redeemed, since we have exceptions in St. Severinus and St. Paschal, as related in a legend.

30. No one is sure of the integrity of his own contrition, much less of having received plenary remission.

31. The man who actually buys indulgences is as rare as he who is really penitent; indeed, he is exceedingly rare.

32. Those who believe that they can be certain of their salvation because they have indulgence letters will be eternally damned, together with their teachers.

33. Men must especially be on their guard against those who say that the pope's pardons are that inestimable gift of God by which man is reconciled to him.

34. For the graces of indulgences are concerned only with the penalties of sacramental satisfaction established by man.

35. They who teach that contrition is not necessary on the part of those who intend to buy souls out of purgatory or to buy confessional privileges preach unchristian doctrine.

36. Any truly repentant Christian has a right to full remission of penalty and guilt, even without indulgence letters.

37. Any true Christian, whether living or dead, participates in all the blessings of Christ and the church; and this is granted him by God, even without indulgence letters.

38. Nevertheless, papal remission and blessing are by no means to be disregarded, for they are, as I have said [Thesis 6], the proclamation of the divine remission.

39. It is very difficult, even for the most learned theologians, at one and the same time to commend to the people the bounty of indulgences and the need of true contrition.

40. A Christian who is truly contrite seeks and loves to pay penalties for his sins; the bounty of indulgences, however, relaxes penalties and causes men to hate them—at least it furnishes occasion for hating them.

41. Papal indulgences must be preached with caution, lest people erroneously think that they are preferable to other good works of love.

42. Christians are to be taught that the pope does not intend that the buying of indulgences should in any way be compared with works of mercy.

43. Christians are to be taught that he who gives to the poor or lends to the needy does a better deed than he who buys indulgences.

44. Because love grows by works of love, man thereby becomes better. Man does not, however, become better by means of indulgences but is merely freed from penalties.

45. Christians are to be taught that he who sees a needy man and passes him by, yet gives his money for indulgences, does not buy papal indulgences, but God's wrath.

46. Christians are to be taught that unless they have more

than they need, they must reserve enough for their family needs and by no means squander it on indulgences.

47. Christians are to be taught that the buying of indulgences is a matter of free choice, not commanded.

48. Christians are to be taught that the pope, in granting indulgences, needs and thus desires their devout prayer more than their money.

49. Christians are to be taught that papal indulgences are useful only if they do not put their trust in them, but very harmful if they lose their fear of God because of them.

50. Christians are to be taught that if the pope knew the exactions of the indulgence preachers, he would rather that the basilica of St. Peter were burned to ashes than built up with the skin, flesh and bones of his sheep.

51. Christians are to be taught that the pope would and should wish to give of his own money, even though he had to sell the basilica of St. Peter, to many of those from whom certain hawkers of indulgences cajole money.

52. It is vain to trust in salvation by indulgence letters, even though the indulgence commissary, or even the pope, were to offer his soul as security.

53. The enemies of Christ and the pope who forbid altogether the preaching of the Word of God in some churches in order that indulgences may be preached in others.

54. Injury is done the Word of God when, in the same sermon, an equal or larger amount of time is devoted to indulgences than to the Word.

55. It is certainly the pope's sentiment that if indulgences, which are a very insignificant thing, are celebrated with one bell, one procession, and one ceremony, then the gospel, which is the very greatest thing, should be preached with a hundred bells, a hundred processions, a hundred ceremonies.

56. The treasures of the church, out of which the pope distributes indulgences, are not sufficiently discussed or known among the people of Christ.

57. That indulgences are not temporal treasures is certainly clear, for many indulgence sellers do not distribute them freely but only gather them.

58. Nor are they the merits of Christ and the saints, for, even without the pope, the latter always work grace for the inner man, and the cross, death, and hell for the outer man.

59. St. Laurence said that the poor of the church were the treasures of the church, but he spoke according to the usage of the word in his own time.

60. Without want of consideration we say that the keys of the church, given by the merits of Christ, are that treasure.

61. For it is clear that the pope's power is of itself sufficient for the remission of penalties and cases reserved by himself.

62. The true treasure of the church is the most holy gospel of the glory and grace of God.

63. But this treasure is naturally most odious, for it makes the first to be the last [Matt. 20:16].

64. On the other hand, the treasure of indulgences is naturally most acceptable, for it makes the last to be first.

65. Therefore the treasures of the gospel are nets with which one formerly fished for men of wealth.

66. The treasures of indulgences are nets with which one now fishes for the wealth of men.

67. The indulgences which the demagogues acclaim as the greatest graces are actually understood to be such only insofar as they promote gain.

68. They are nevertheless in truth the most insignificant graces when compared with the grace of God and the piety of the cross.

69. Bishops and curates are bound to admit the commissaries of papal indulgences with all reverence.

70. But they are much more bound to strain their eyes and ears lest these men preach their own dreams instead of what the pope has commissioned.

71. Let him who speaks against the truth concerning papal indulgences be anathema and accursed;

72. But let him who guards against the lust and license of the indulgence preachers be blessed;

73. Just as the pope justly thunders against those who by any means whatsoever contrive harm to the sale of indulgences.

74. But much more does he intend to thunder against those

who use indulgences as a pretext to contrive harm to holy love and truth.

75. To consider papal indulgences so great that they could absolve a man even if he had done the impossible and had violated the mother of God is madness.

76. We say on the contrary that papal indulgences cannot remove the very least of venial sins as far as guilt is concerned.

77. To say that even St. Peter, if he were now pope, could not grant greater graces is blasphemy against St. Peter and the pope.

78. We say on the contrary that even the present pope, or any pope whatsoever, has greater graces at his disposal, that is the gospel, spiritual powers, gifts of healing, etc., as it is written in I. Cor. 12 [:28].

79. To say that the cross emblazoned with the papal coat of arms and set up by the indulgence preachers is equal in worth to the cross of Christ is blasphemy.

80. The bishops, curates and theologians who permit such talk to be spread among the people will have to answer for this.

81. This unbridled preaching of indulgences makes it difficult even for learned men to rescue the reverence which is due the pope from slander or from the shrewd questions of the laity.

82. Such as: "Why does not the pope empty purgatory for the sake of holy love and the dire need of the souls that are there if he redeems an infinite number of souls for the sake of miserable money with which to build a church? The former reasons would be most just; the latter is most trivial."

83. Again, "Why are funeral and anniversary masses for the dead continued and why does he not return or permit the withdrawal of the endowments founded for them, since it is wrong to pray for the redeemed?"

84. Again, "What is this new piety of God and the pope that for a consideration of money they permit a man who is impious and their enemy to buy out of purgatory the pious soul of a friend of God and do not rather, because of the need of that pious and beloved soul, free it for pure love's sake?"

85.   Again, "Why are the penitential canons, long since abrogated and dead in actual fact and through disuse, now satisfied by the granting of indulgences as though they were still alive and in force?"

86.   Again, "Why does not the pope, whose wealth is today greater than the wealth of the richest Crassus, build this one basilica of St. Peter with his own money rather than with the money of poor believers?"

87.   Again, "What does the pope remit or grant to those who by perfect contrition already have a right to full remission and blessings?"

88.   Again, "What greater blessing could come to the church than if the pope were to bestow these remissions and blessings on every believer a hundred times a day, as he now does but once?"

89.   "Since the pope seeks the salvation of souls rather than money by his indulgences, why does he suspend the indulgences and pardons previously granted when they have equal efficacy?"

90.   To repress these very sharp arguments of the laity by force alone, and not to resolve them by giving reasons, is to expose the church and the pope to the ridicule of their enemies and to make Christians unhappy.

91.   If, therefore, indulgences were preached according to the spirit and intention of the pope, all these doubts would be readily resolved. Indeed, they would not exist.

92.   Away then with all those prophets who say to the people of Christ, "Peace, peace," and there is no peace! [Jer. 6:14].

93.   Blessed be all those prophets who say to the people of Christ, "Cross, cross," and there is no cross!

94.   Christians should be exhorted to be diligent in following Christ their Head through penalties, death, and hell;

95.   And thus be confident of entering into heaven through many tribulations rather than through the false security of peace [Acts 14:22].

3. Luther: An Appeal to the Ruling Class of German Nationality as to the Amelioration of the State of Christendom

Within a period of six months Luther published his famous three Reformation treatises of 1520. On August 18 he published *An Appeal to the Ruling Class,* an open letter to the Christians in authority to undertake the reform which the church had failed to make. Indignation at the baseness of the Renaissance papacy and anger at the exploitation of the Germans by the Roman church, reminiscent of Hutten's assaults, are voiced sharply in this address. The *Appeal,* which has been called a "cry from the heart of the people" and a "blast on the war-trumpet," was Luther's first writing after he was convinced that his breach with Rome was all but irreparable. He followed it with *On the Babylonian Captivity of the Church,* October 6, attacking the use of the sacramental system for hierarchical control of Christians, and with his *Treatise on Christian Liberty,* published early in November. From Bertram Lee Woolf, ed., *Reformation Writings of Martin Luther,* I, *The Basis of the Protestant Reformation* (New York: Philosophical Library, 1953), pp. 109, 110-115, 119-120, 121-125. Reprinted by permission of the publishers.

Doctor Martin Luther to His Most Illustrious, Most Mighty and Imperial Majesty, and to the Christians of the German ruling Class.

Grace and power from God to His Illustrious Majesty, and to you, most gracious and honorable Gentlemen.

It is not due to sheer impertinence or wantonness that I, a lone and simple man, have taken it upon myself to address your worships. All classes in Christendom, particularly in Germany, are now oppressed by distress and affliction, and this has stirred not only me but every man to cry out anxiously for help. It has compelled me to beg and pray that God will endow someone with His Spirit to bring aid to this unhappy nation. Proposals have often been made at councils, but have been cunningly deferred by the guile of certain men, and matters have gone from bad to worse. Their artifices and wickedness I intend with God's help to lay bare in order that, once shown up, they may never again present such hindrances or be so harmful. God has given us a young man of noble ancestry to be our head and so has raised high hopes in many hearts. In these circumstances, it is fitting for us to do all we can to make good use of the present time and of God's gracious gift to us.

The first and most urgent thing just now is that we should each prepare our own selves in all seriousness. We must not begin by assuming we possess much strength or wisdom, even if we had all the authority in the world. For God cannot and will not suffer a goodly enterprise to be begun if we trust in our own strength and wisdom. God will surely abase such pride, as is said in Psalm 33 [:16], "No king stands by the multitude of his host, and no lord by the greatness of his strength." For this reason, I fear, it came to pass in former times that the good princes, Emperors Frederick I and II, and many other German emperors, were shamelessly trodden under foot and oppressed by the popes whom all the world feared. Perhaps they relied more on their own strength than on God, and therefore had to fall. And what else, in our day, has raised the bloodthirsty Julius II so high, if it were not, as I fear, that France, Germany, and Venice depended on themselves? The children of Benjamin slew 42,000 Israelites because they relied on their own strength.

Lest we have the same experience under our noble Emperor, Charles, we must be clear that we are not dealing permanently with men in this matter, but with the princes of hell who would fill the world with war and bloodshed, and yet avoid letting themselves be caught by the flood. We must go to work now, not depending on physical power, but in humble trust in God, seeking help from Him in earnest prayer, with nothing else in mind than the misery and distress of all Christendom suffering over and above what sinful men have deserved. Otherwise our efforts may well begin with good prospects, but, when we get deeply involved, the evil spirit will cause such confusion as to make the whole world swim in blood, and then nothing will be accomplished. Therefore in this matter let us act wisely, and as those who fear God. The greater the power we employ, the greater the disaster we suffer, unless we act humbly and in the fear of God. If hitherto, the popes and Romanists have been able, with the devil's help, to bring kings into conflict with each other, they will be able to do it again now, if we set forth without God's help and armed only with our own strength and shrewdness.

The Three Walls

The Romanists have very cleverly surrounded themselves with three walls, which have protected them till now in such a way that no one could reform them. As a result, the whole of Christendom has suffered woeful corruption. In the first place, when under the threat of secular force, they have stood firm and declared that secular force had no jurisdiction over them; rather the opposite was the case, and the spiritual was superior to the secular. In the second place, when the Holy Scriptures have been used to reprove them, they have responded that no one except the pope was competent to expound Scripture. In the third place, when threatened with a council, they have pretended that no one but the pope could summon a council. In this way they have adroitly nullified these three means of correction, and avoided punishment. Thus they still remain in secure possession of these three walls, and practice all the villainy and wickedness we see today. When they have been compelled to hold a council, they have made it nugatory by compelling the princes to swear in advance that the present position shall remain undisturbed. In addition, they have given the pope full authority over all the decisions of a council, till it is a matter of indifference whether there be many councils or none; for they only deceive us with make-believes and sham fights. So terribly fearful are they for their skins, if a truly free council were held. Further, the Romanists have overawed kings and princes till the latter believe it would be impious not to obey them in spite of all the deceitful and cunning dodges of theirs.

May God now help us and give us one of those trumpets with

which the walls of Jericho were overthrown; that we may blow away these walls of paper and straw, and set free the Christian, corrective measures to punish sin and to bring the devil's deceits and wiles to the light of day. In this way, may we be reformed through suffering and again receive God's blessing.

I. LET US BEGIN BY ATTACKING THE FIRST WALL

To call popes, bishops, priests, monks and nuns the religious class, but princes, lords, artisans and farm-workers the secular class is a specious device invented by certain time-servers; but no one ought to be frightened by it, and for good reason. For all Christians whatsoever really and truly belong to the religious class, and there is no difference among them except insofar as they do different work. That is St. Paul's meaning in I Corinthians 12 [:12 f.], when he says: "We are all one body, yet each member hath his own work for serving others." This applies to us all, because we have one baptism, one gospel, one faith, and are all equally Christian. For baptism, gospel, and faith alone make men religious and create a Christian people. When a pope or bishop anoints, grants tonsures, ordains, consecrates, dresses differently from laymen, he may make a hypocrite of a man, or an anointed image, but never a Christian or a spiritually-minded man. The fact is that our baptism consecrates us all without exception and makes us all priests. As St. Peter says, I Pet. 2 [:9], "You are a royal priesthood and a realm of priests," and Revelation, "Thou hast made us priests and kings by Thy blood" [Rev. 5:9 f.]. If we ourselves as Christians did not receive a higher consecration than that given by pope or bishop, then no one would be made priest even by consecration at the hands of pope or bishop; nor would anyone be authorized to celebrate Eucharist, or preach, or pronounce absolution.

When a bishop consecrates, he simply acts on behalf of the entire congregation, all of whom have the same authority. They may select one of their number and command him to exercise this authority on behalf of the others. It would be similar if ten brothers, king's sons and equal heirs, were to choose one of themselves to rule the kingdom for them. All would be kings and of equal authority, although one was appointed to rule. To put it more plainly, suppose a small group of earnest Christian laymen were taken prisoner and settled in the middle of a desert without any episcopally ordained priest among them; and they then agreed to choose one of themselves, whether married or not, and endow him with the office of baptizing, administering the sacrament, pronouncing absolution and preaching; that man would be as truly a priest as if he had been ordained by all the bishops and the popes. It follows that, if needs be, anyone may baptize or pronounce absolution, an impossible situation if we were not all priests. The fact that baptism, and the Christian status which it confers, possess such great grace and authority, is what the Romanists have overridden by their canon law and kept us in ignorance thereof. But in former days Christians used to choose their bishops and priests from their own members, and these were afterwards confirmed by other bishops without any of the pomp of present custom. St. Augustine, Ambrose, and Cyprian each became bishops in this way.

Those who exercise secular authority have been baptized like the rest of us, and have the same faith and the same gospel; therefore we must admit that they are priests and bishops. They discharge their office as an office of the Christian community and for the benefit of that community. Everyone who has been baptized may claim that he has already been consecrated priest, bishop, or pope, even though it is not seemly for any particular person arbitrarily to exercise the office. Just because we are all priests of equal standing, no one must push himself forward and, without the consent and choice of the rest, presume to do that for which we all have authority. Only by the consent and command of the community should any individual person claim for himself what belongs equally to all. If it should happen that anyone abuses an office for which he has been chosen, and is dismissed for that reason, he would resume his former status. It follows that the status of a priest among Christians is merely that of an office-bearer; while he holds the office he exercises it; if he be deposed he resumes his status in the community and becomes like the rest. Certainly a priest is no longer a priest after being unfrocked. Yet the Romanists have devised the claim to *characteres indelebiles,* and assert that a priest, even if deposed, is different from a mere layman. They even hold the illusion that a priest can never be anything else than a priest, and therefore never a layman again. All these are human inventions and regulations. . . .

II.

The second wall is more loosely built and less indefensible. The Romanists profess to be the only interpreters of Scripture, even though they never learn anything contained in it their lives long. They claim authority for themselves alone, juggle . . . words shamelessly before our eyes, saying that the pope cannot err as to the faith, whether he be bad or good, although they cannot quote a single letter of Scripture to support their claim. Thus it comes about that so many heretical, unchristian, and even unnatural laws are contained in the canon law—matters of which there is no need for discussion at the present juncture. Just because the Romanists profess to believe that the Holy Spirit has not abandoned them, no matter if they are as ignorant and bad as they could be, they presume to assert whatever they please. In such a case, what is the need or the value of Holy Scripture? Let it be burned, and let us be content with the ignorant gentlemen at Rome who "possess the Holy Spirit within," [who], however, in fact, dwells in pious souls only. Had I not read it, I should have thought it incredible that the devil should have produced such ineptitudes at Rome, and have gained adherents to them. But lest we fight them with mere words, let us adduce Scripture. St. Paul says, I Corinthians 14 [:30], "If something superior be revealed to any one sitting there and listening to another speaking God's word, the first speaker must be silent and give place." What would be the virtue of this commandment if only the speaker, or the person in the highest position, were to be believed? Christ Himself says, John 6 [:45], "that all Christians shall be taught by God." Then if the pope and his adherents were bad men and not true Christians, i.e., not taught by God to have a true understanding; and if, on the other hand, a humble person should have the true understanding, why ever should we not follow him? Has not the pope made many errors? Who could enlighten Christian people if the pope erred, unless someone else, who had the support of Scripture, were more to be believed than he?

Therefore it is a wicked, base invention, for which they cannot adduce a tittle of evidence in support, to aver that it is the function of the pope alone to interpret Scripture or to confirm any particular interpretation. And if they claim that St. Peter received authority when he was given the keys—well, it is plain enough that the keys were not given to St. Peter only, but to the whole Christian community. Moreover the keys have no reference to doctrine or policy, but only to refusing or being willing to forgive sin. . . .

III.

The third wall falls without more ado when the first two are demolished; for, even if the pope acts contrary to Scripture, we ourselves are bound to abide by Scripture. We must punish him and constrain him, according to the passage, "If thy brother sin against thee, go and tell it him between thee and him alone; but if he hear thee not, take with thee one or two more; and if he hear them not, tell it to the church; and if he hear not the church, let him be unto thee as a Gentile" [Matt. 18:15-17]. This passage commands each member to exercise concern for his fellow; much more is it our duty when the wrongdoer is one who rules over us all alike, and who causes much harm and offence to the rest by his conduct. And if I am to lay a charge against him before the church, then I must call it together.

Romanists have no Scriptural basis for their contention that the pope alone has the right to summon or sanction a council. This is their own ruling, and valid only as long as it is not harmful to Christian well-being or contrary to God's laws. If, however, the pope is in the wrong, this ruling becomes invalid, because it is harmful to Christian well-being not to punish him through a council.

Accordingly, we read in Acts 15 [:6] that it was not St. Peter, but all the apostles and elders, who called the Apostolic Council. If that had been the sole right of St. Peter, it would not have been a Christian council but an heretical *conciliabulum*. Further, the bishop of Rome neither called nor sanctioned the council of Nicea, the most celebrated of all, but the Emperor, Constantine. After him, many other emperors did the same, and these councils were the most Christian of all. But if the pope had really had the sole authority, then they would necessarily all have been heretical. Moreover, when I examine decisions of those councils which the pope himself called, I find they did nothing of special importance.

Therefore, when need requires it, and the pope is acting harm-

fully to Christian well-being, let anyone who is a true member of
the Christian community as a whole take steps as early as possible
to bring about a genuinely free council. No one is so able to do
this as the secular authorities, especially since they are also fellow Christians, fellow priests, similarly religious, and of similar
authority in all respects. They should exercise their office and do
their work without let or hindrance where it is necessary or ad-
vantageous to do so, for God has given them authority over everyone. Surely it would be an unnatural proceeding, if fire were to
break out in a town, if everyone should stand still and let it burn
on and on, simply because no one had the mayor's authority, or
perhaps because it began at the mayor's residence. In such a case,
is it not the duty of each citizen to stir up the rest and call upon
them for help? Much more ought it to be the case in the spiritual
city of Christ, were a fire of offence to break out, whether in the
pope's regime or anywhere else. The same argument would hold
if an enemy were to attack a town; that man who called his
fellow citizens together at the earliest moment would deserve
honor and gratitude. Why then should not honor be accorded to
one who makes our infernal enemies known, rouses Christian
people and calls them together?

It is empty talk when the Romanists boast of possessing an
authority such as cannot properly be contested. No one in Christendom has authority to do evil or to forbid evil from being resisted.
The church has no authority except to promote the greater good.
Hence, if the pope should exercise his authority to prevent a free
council, and so hinder the reform of the church, we ought to pay
no regard to him and his authority. If he should excommunicate
and fulminate, that ought to be despised as the proceedings of a
foolish man. Trusting in God's protection, we ought to excommunicate him in return and manage as best we can; for this
authority of his would be presumptuous and empty. He does not
possess it, and he would fall an easy victim to a passage of Scripture; for Paul says to the Corinthians, "For God gave us authority,
not to cast down Christendom, but to build it up" [II Cor. 10:8].
Who would pretend to ignore this text? Only the power of the
devil and the Antichrist attempting to arrest whatever serves the
reform of Christendom. Wherefore, we must resist that power
with life and limb, and might and main.

Even if some supernatural sign should be given, and appear to support the pope against the secular authority; e.g., if a plague were to strike someone down, as they boast has happened sometimes, we ought only to regard it as caused by the devil on account of our lack of faith in God. It is what Christ proclaimed, "False Christs and false prophets will come in my name, and will do signs and wonders, so as to lead astray, if possible, even the elect" [Matt. 24:24]. St. Paul says to the Thessalonians [II Thess. 2:9] that the Antichrist shall, through Satan, be mighty in false, miraculous signs. . . .

And now, I hope that I have [allayed] these false and deceptive terrors, though the Romanists have long used them to make us diffident and of a fearful conscience. It is obvious to all that they, like us, are subject to the authority of the state, that they have no warrant to expound Scripture arbitrarily and without special knowledge. They are not empowered to prohibit a council or, according to their pleasure, to determine its decisions in advance, to bind it and to rob it of freedom. But if they do so, I hope I have shown that of a truth they belong to the community of Antichrist and the devil, and have nothing in common with Christ except the name.

4. Luther: Treatise on Christian Liberty

Luther's third famous treatise of 1520 was devotional in nature and, in his words, contained "the whole of Christian life in brief form." In it Luther undertook to describe the liberating effect of faith in Christ upon the Christian man: faith which frees him from spiritual slavery and moves him to a life of love and service to God and man. Conciliatory in love, the *Treatise* was accompanied by an open letter to Pope Leo affirming that Luther's intention had been to attack the false doctrines and corruption surrounding the papacy and not Leo's own person. The following year Luther made his stand at the Diet at Worms before the Emperor, Imperial Estates, and Papal emissaries in what the English historian James A.

Many people have considered Christian faith an easy thing, and not a few have given it a place among the virtues. They do this because they have not experienced it and have never tasted the great strength there is in faith. It is impossible to write well about it or to understand what has been written about it unless one has at one time or another experienced the courage which faith gives a man when trials oppress him. But he who has had even a faint taste of it can never write, speak, meditate, or hear enough concerning it. It is a living "spring of water welling up to eternal life," as Christ calls it in John 4 [:14].

As for me, although I have no wealth of faith to boast of and know how scant my supply is, I nevertheless hope that I have attained to a little faith, even though I have been assailed by great and various temptations; and I hope that I can discuss it, if not more elegantly, certainly more to the point, than those literalists and subtle disputants have previously done, who have not even understood what they have written.

To make the way smoother for the unlearned—for only them do I serve—I shall set down the following two propositions concerning the freedom and the bondage of the spirit:

A Christian is a perfectly free lord of all, subject to none.

A Christian is a perfectly dutiful servant of all, subject to all.

These two theses seem to contradict each other. If, however, they should be found to fit together they would serve our purpose beautifully. Both are Paul's own statements, who says in I Cor. 9 [:19], "For though I am free from all men, I have made myself a slave to all," and in Rom. 13 [:8], "Owe no one anything, except to love one another." Love by its very nature is ready to serve and be subject to him who is loved. So Christ, although he was Lord of all, was "born of woman, born under the law" [Gal. 4:4], and therefore was at the same time a free man and a servant, "in the form of God" and "of a servant" [Phil. 2:6-7].

Let us start, however, with something more remote from our subject, but more obvious. Man has a twofold nature, a spiritual and a bodily one. According to the spiritual nature, which men refer to as the soul, he is called a spiritual, inner, or new man. According to the bodily nature, which men refer to as flesh, he is called a carnal, outward, or old man, of whom the Apostle writes in II Cor. 4 [:16], "Though our outer nature is wasting away our inner nature is being renewed every day." Because of this diversity of nature the Scriptures assert contradictory things concerning the same man, since these two men in the same man contradict each other, "for the desires of the flesh are against the Spirit, and the desires of the Spirit are against the flesh," according to Gal. 5:17.

First, let us consider the inner man to see how a righteous, free, and pious Christian, that is, a spiritual, new, and inner man, becomes what he is. It is evident that no external thing has any influence in producing Christian righteousness or freedom, or in producing unrighteousness or servitude. A simple argument will furnish the proof of this statement. What can it profit the soul if the body is well, free and active, and eats, drinks and does as it pleases? For in these respects even the most godless slaves of vice may prosper. On the other hand, how will poor health or imprisonment or hunger or thirst or any other external misfortune harm the soul? Even the most godly men, and those who are free because of clear consciences, are afflicted with these things. None of these things touches either the freedom or the servitude of the soul. It does not help the soul if the body is adorned with the sacred robes of priests or dwells in sacred places or is occupied with sacred duties or prays, fasts, abstains from certain kinds of food, or does any work that can be done by the body and in the body. The righteousness and the freedom of the soul require something far different since the things which have been mentioned could be done by any wicked person. Such works produce nothing but hypocrites. On the other hand, it will not harm the soul if the body is clothed in secular dress, dwells in unconsecrated places, eats and drinks as others do, does not pray aloud, and neglects to do all the above-mentioned things which hypocrites can do.

Furthermore, to put aside all kinds of works, even contemplation, meditation, and all that the soul can do, does not help. One thing, and only one thing, is necessary for Christian life, righteousness, and freedom. That one thing is the most holy Word of God, the Gospel of Christ, as Christ says, John II [:25], "I am the resurrection and the life; he who believes in me, though he die, yet shall he live"; and John 8 [:36], "So if the Son makes you free, you will be free indeed"; and Matt. 4 [:4], "Man shall not live by bread alone, but by every word that proceeds from the mouth of God." Let us then consider it certain and firmly established that the soul can do without anything except the Word of God and that where the Word of God is missing there is no help at all for the soul. If it has the Word of God it is rich and lacks nothing since it is the Word of life, truth, light, peace, righteousness, salvation, joy, liberty, wisdom, power, grace, glory, and of every incalculable blessing. This is why the prophet in the entire Psalm [119] and in many other places yearns and sighs for the Word of God and uses so many names to describe it.

On the other hand, there is no more terrible disaster with which the wrath of God can afflict men than a famine of the hearing of His Word, as He says in Amos [8:11]. Likewise there is no greater mercy than when He sends forth His Word, as we read in Psalm 107 [:20]: "He sent forth His word, and healed them, and delivered them from destruction." Nor was Christ sent into the world for any other ministry except that of the Word. Moreover, the entire spiritual estate—all the apostles, bishops, and priests—has been called and instituted only for the ministry of the Word.

You may ask, "What then is the Word of God, and how shall it be used, since there are so many words of God?" I answer: The Apostle explains this in Romans 1. The Word is the Gospel of God concerning his Son, Who was made flesh, suffered, rose from the dead, and was glorified through the Spirit who sanctifies. To preach Christ means to feed the soul, make it righteous, set it free and save it, provided it believes the preaching. Faith alone is the saving and efficacious use of the Word of God, according to Rom. 10 [:9]: "If you confess with your lips that Jesus is Lord and believe in your heart that God raised Him from the dead, you will be saved." Furthermore, "Christ is the end of the law, that every one who has faith may be justified" [Rom. 10:4]. Again, in Rom. 1 [:17], "He who through faith is righteous shall live." The Word of God cannot be received and cherished by any works whatever but only by faith. Therefore it is clear that, as the soul needs only the Word of God for its life and righteousness, so it is justified by faith alone and not any works; for if it could be justified by anything else, it would not need the Word, and consequently it would not need faith. . . .

Should you ask how it happens that faith alone justifies and offers us such a treasure of great benefits without works in view of the fact that so many works, ceremonies, and laws are prescribed in the Scriptures, I answer: First of all, remember what has been said, namely, that faith alone, without works, justifies, frees and saves; we shall make this clearer later on. Here we must point out that the entire Scripture of God is divided into two parts: commandments and promises. Although the commandments teach things that are good, the things taught are not done as soon as they are taught, for the commandments show us what we ought to do but do not give us the power to do it. They are intended to teach man to know himself, that through them he may recognize his inability to do good and may despair of his own ability. That is why they are called the Old Testament and constitute the Old Testament. For example, the commandment, "You shall not covet" [Exod. 20:17], is a command which proves us all to be sinners, for no one can avoid coveting no matter how much he may struggle against it. Therefore, in order not to covet and to fulfill the commandment, a man is compelled to despair of himself, to seek the help which he does not find in himself elsewhere and from someone else, as stated in Hosea [13:9]: "Destruction is your own, O Israel: your help is only in me." As we fare with respect to one commandment, so we fare with all, for it is equally impossible for us to keep any one of them.

Now when a man has learned through the commandments to recognize his helplessness and is distressed about how he might satisfy the law—since the law must be fulfilled so that not a jot or tittle shall be lost, otherwise man will be condemned without hope—then, being truly humbled and reduced to nothing in his own eyes, he finds in himself nothing whereby he may be justified and saved. Here the second part of Scripture comes to our aid, namely, the promises of God which declare the glory of God, saying, "If you wish to fulfill the law and not covet, as the law demands, come, believe in Christ in whom grace, righteousness, peace, liberty, and all things are promised you. If you believe, you shall have all things; if you do not believe, you shall lack all things." That which is impossible for you to accomplish by trying to fulfill all the works of the law—many and useless as they all are—you will accomplish quickly and easily through faith. God our Father has made all things depend on faith so that whoever has faith will have everything, and whoever does not have faith will have nothing. "For God has consigned all men to disobedience, that he may have mercy upon all," as stated in Rom. II [:32]. Thus the promises of God give what the commandments of God demand and fulfill what the law prescribes so that all things may be God's alone, both the commandments and the fulfilling of the commandments. He alone commands, He alone fulfills. Therefore the promises of God belong to the New Testament. Indeed, they are the New Testament.

Since these promises of God are holy, true, righteous, free and peaceful words, full of goodness, the soul which clings to them with a firm faith will be so closely united with them and altogether absorbed by them that it not only will share in all their power but will be saturated and intoxicated by them. If a touch of Christ healed, how much more will this most tender spiritual touch, this absorbing of the Word, communicate to the soul all things that belong to the Word. This, then, is how through faith alone without works the soul is justified by the Word of God, sanctified, made true, peaceful and free, filled with every blessing and truly made a child of God, as John I [:12] says: "But to all who . . . believed in his name, he gave power to become children of God."

From what has been said it is easy to see from what source faith derives such great power and why a good work or all good works together cannot equal it. No good work can rely upon the Word of God or live in the soul, for faith alone and the Word of God rule in the soul. Just as the heated iron glows like fire because of the union of fire with it, so the Word imparts its qualities to the soul. It is clear, then, that a Christian has all that he needs in faith and needs no works to justify him; and if he has no need of works, he has no need of the law; and if he has no need of the law, surely he is free from the law. It is true that "the law is not laid down for the just" [I Tim. 1:9]. This is that Christian liberty, our faith, which does not induce us to live in idleness or wickedness but makes the law and works unnecessary for any man's righteousness and salvation . . .

Not only are we the freest of kings, we are also priests forever, which is far more excellent than being kings, for as priests we are worthy to appear before God to pray for others and to teach one another divine things. These are the functions of priests, and they cannot be granted to any unbeliever. Thus Christ has made it possible for us, provided we believe in Him, to be not only His brethren, co-heirs and fellow-kings, but also His fellow-priests. Therefore we may boldly come into the presence of God in the spirit of faith [Heb. 10:19, 22] and cry "Abba, Father!" [We may] pray for one another, and do all things which we see done and foreshadowed in the outer and visible works of priests. . . .

You will ask, "If all who are in the church are priests, how do these whom we now call priests differ from laymen?" I answer: Injustice is done those words "priest," "cleric," "spiritual," "ecclesiastic," when they are transferred from all Christians to those few who are now by a mischievous usage called "ecclesiastics." Holy Scripture makes no distinction between them, although it gives the name "ministers," "servants," "stewards" to those who are now proudly called popes, bishops, and lords and who should according to the ministry of the Word serve others and teach them the faith of Christ and the freedom of believers. Although we are all equally priests, we cannot all publicly minister and teach. We ought not do so even if we could. Paul writes accordingly in I Cor. 4 [1], "This is how one should regard us, as servants of Christ and stewards of the mysteries of God." . . .

To return to our purpose, I believe that it has now become clear that it is not enough or in any sense Christian to preach the works, life and words of Christ as historical facts, as if the knowledge of these would suffice for the conduct of life; yet this is the fashion among those who must today be regarded as our best preachers. Far less is it sufficient or Christian to say nothing at all about Christ and to teach instead the laws of men and the decrees of the fathers. Now there are not a few who preach Christ and read about Him that they may move men's affections to sympathy with Christ, to anger against the Jews, and such childish and effeminate nonsense. Rather ought Christ to be preached to the end that faith in Him may be established that He may not only be Christ, but be Christ for you and me, and that what is said of Him and is denoted in His name may be effectual in us. Such faith is produced and preserved in us by preaching why Christ came, what He brought and bestowed, what benefit it is to us to accept Him. This is done when that Christian liberty which He bestows is rightly taught and we are told in what way we Christians are all kings and priests and therefore lords of all and may firmly believe that whatever we have done is pleasing and acceptable in the sight of God, as I have already said.

What man is there whose heart, upon hearing these things, will not rejoice to its depth, and when receiving such comfort will not grow tender so that he will love Christ as he never could by means of any laws or works? Who would have the power to harm or frighten such a heart? If the knowledge of sin or the fear of death should break in upon it, it is ready to hope in the Lord. It does not grow afraid when it hears tidings of evil. It is not disturbed when it sees its enemies. This is so because it believes that the righteousness of Christ is its own and that its sin is not its own, but Christ's, and that all sin is swallowed up by the righteousness of Christ. This, as has been said above, is a necessary consequence . . . of faith in Christ. So the heart learns to scoff at death and sin and to say with the Apostle, "O death, where is thy victory? O death, where is thy sting? The sting of death is sin, and the power of sin is the law. But thanks be to God, who gives us the victory through our Lord Jesus Christ" [I Cor. 15:55-57]. Death is swallowed up not only in the victory of Christ but also by our victory, because through faith His victory has become ours and in that faith we also are conquerors.

Let this suffice concerning the inner man, his liberty, and the source of his liberty, the righteousness of faith. He needs neither laws nor good works but, on the contrary, is injured by them if he believes that he is justified by them.

Now let us turn to the second part, the outer man. Here we shall answer all those who, offended by the word "faith" and by all that has been said, now ask, "If faith does all things and is alone sufficient unto righteousness, why then are good works commanded? We will take our ease and do no works and be content with faith." I answer: not so, you wicked men, not so. That would indeed be proper if we were wholly inner and perfectly spiritual men. But such we shall be only at the last day, the day of the resurrection of the dead. As long as we live in the flesh we only begin to make some progress in that which shall be perfected in the future life. For this reason the Apostle in Rom. 8 [:23] calls all that we attain in this life "the first fruits of the Spirit" because we shall indeed receive the greater portion, even the fullness of the Spirit, in the future. This is the place to assert [what] was said above, namely, that a Christian is the servant of all and made subject to all. Insofar as he is free he does no works, but insofar as he is a servant he does all kinds of works. . . .

In doing these works, however, we must not think that a man is justified before God by them, for faith, which alone is righteousness before God, cannot endure that erroneous opinion. We must, however, realize that these works reduce the body to subjection and purify it of its evil lusts, and our whole purpose is to be directed only toward the driving out of lusts. Since by faith the soul is cleansed and made to love God, it desires that all things, and especially its own body, shall be purified so that all things may join with it in loving and praising God. Hence a man cannot be idle, for the need of his body drives him and he is compelled to do many good works to reduce it to subjection. Nevertheless the works themselves do not justify him before God, but he does the works out of spontaneous love in obedience to God and considers nothing except the approval of God, whom he would most scrupulously obey in all things. . . .

The following statements are therefore true: "Good works do not make a good man, but a good man does good works; evil works do not make a wicked man, but a wicked man does evil works." Consequently it is always necessary that the substance or person himself be good before there can be any good works, and that good works follow and proceed from the good person, as Christ also says, "A good tree cannot bear evil fruit, nor can a bad tree bear good fruit" [Matt. 7:18]. It is clear that the fruits do not bear the tree and that the tree does not grow on the fruits; also that, on the contrary, the trees bear the fruits and the fruits grow on the trees. As it is necessary, therefore, that the trees exist before their fruits and the fruits do not make trees either good or bad, but rather as the trees are, so are the fruits they bear; so a man must first be good or wicked before he does a good or wicked work, and his works do not make him good or wicked, but he himself makes his works either good or wicked. . . .

Since human nature and natural reason, as it is called, are by nature superstitious and ready to imagine, when laws and works are prescribed, that righteousness must be obtained through laws and works; and further, since they are trained and confirmed in this opinion by the practice of all earthly lawgivers, it is im-

possible that they should of themselves escape from the slavery
of works and come to a knowledge of the freedom of faith. Therefore there is need of the prayer that the Lord may give us and
make us *theodidacti*, that is, those taught by God [John 6:45];
and Himself, as He has promised, write His law in our hearts.
Otherwise there is no hope for us. If He Himself does not teach
our hearts this wisdom hidden in mystery [I Cor. 2:7], nature can
only condemn it and judge it to be heretical because nature is
offended by it and regards it as foolishness. So . . . it happened
in the old days in the case of the apostles and prophets, and so
godless and blind popes and their flatterers do to me and to those
who are like me. May God at last be merciful to them and to us
and cause His face to shine upon us that we may know His way
upon earth [Ps. 67:1-2], His salvation among all nations; God,
who is blessed forever [II Cor. 11:31]. Amen.

5. Melanchthon: Funeral Oration Over Luther

Philip Melanchthon (d. 1560) was only twenty-one years old
when he came to the University of Wittenberg in 1518 as professor of Greek in the faculty of liberal arts. He became
Luther's intimate friend and coworker and gave form and
structure to Luther's prophetic utterances. The author of the
Loci Communes (1521) or basic concepts of evangelical theology and the chief formulator of the *Augsburg Confession* (1530)
and the *Apology* or defense of the Augsburg Confession,
Melanchthon was the systematic theologian, scholarly publi-
cist, and ecclesiastical diplomat of early Lutheranism. Melanchthon announced Luther's death to the students at the University with the words: "Alas, gone is the horseman and gone
are the chariots of Israel!" Melanchthon's famous funeral oration is of great interest, for it reveals the way in which he
viewed Luther's role in the history of the church. From James
William Richard, *Philip Melanchthon The Protestant Preceptor of Germany, 1497-1560*. (New York: G. P. Putnam's
Sons, 1898), pp. 381-392.

Though amid the public sorrow my voice is obstructed by grief and tears, yet in this vast assembly something ought to be said, not, as among the heathen, only in praise of the deceased. Much rather is this assembly to be reminded of the wonderful government of the Church, and of her perils, that in our distress we may consider what we are, most of all, to desire, and by what examples we are to regulate our lives. There are ungodly men, who, in the confused condition of human affairs, think that everything is the result of accident. But we who are illumined by the many explicit declarations of God, distinguish the Church from the profane multitude; and we know that it is in reality governed and preserved by God. We fix our eye on this Church. We acknowledge lawful rulers and consider their manner of life. We also select suitable leaders and teachers, whom we may piously follow and reverence.

It is necessary to think on and to speak of these things so often as we name the name of the reverend doctor Martin Luther, our most dear Father and Preceptor, whom many wicked men have most bitterly hated; but whom we, who know that he was a minister of the gospel raised up by God, love and applaud. We also have the evidence to show that his doctrine did not consist of seditious opinions scattered by blind impulse, as men of epicurean tastes suppose; but that it is an exhibition of the will of God and of true worship, an exposition of the Holy Scriptures, a preaching of the Word of God, that is, of the gospel of Jesus Christ.

In orations delivered on occasions like the present, it is the custom to say many things about the personal endowments of those who are panegyrized. But I will omit this and will speak only on the main subject, viz., his relation to the Church; for good men will always judge that if he promoted sound and necessary doctrine in the Church, we should give thanks to God because *He* raised him up; and all good men should praise his labors, fidelity, constancy and other virtues, and should most affectionately cherish his memory.

So much for the exordium of my oration. The Son of God, as Paul observes, sits at the right hand of the Eternal Father and gives gifts unto men, viz., the gospel and the Holy Spirit. That He might bestow these He raises up prophets, apostles, teachers and pastors, and selects from our midst those who study, hear and delight in the writings of the prophets and apostles. Nor does He call into this service only those who occupy the ordinary stations;

but He often makes war upon those very ones by teachers chosen from other stations. It is both pleasant and profitable to contemplate the Church of all ages and to consider the goodness of God in sending useful teachers, one after another, that as some fall in the ranks, others may at once press into their places.

Behold the patriarchs: Adam, Seth, Enoch, Methuselah, Noah, Shem. When in the time of the last named, who lived in the neighborhood of the Sodomites, the nations forgot the teaching of Noah and Shem, and worshipped idols, Abraham was raised up to be Shem's companion and to assist him in his great work and in propagating sound doctrine. He was succeeded by Isaac, Jacob and Joseph, which last lighted the torch of truth in all the land of Egypt, which at that time was the most flourishing kingdom in all the world. Then came Moses, Joshua, Samuel, David, Elijah, Elisha, Isaiah, Jeremiah, Daniel, Zechariah. Then Ezra, Onias, and the Maccabees. Then Simeon, Zacharias, the Baptist, Christ and the apostles. It is a delight to contemplate this unbroken succession, inasmuch as it is a manifest proof of the presence of God in the Church.

After the apostles comes a long line, inferior, indeed, but distinguished by the divine attestations: Polycarp, Irenaeus, Gregory of Neocaesarea, Basil, Augustin, Prosper, Maximus, Hugo, Bernard, Tauler and others. And though these later times have been less fruitful, yet God has always preserved a remnant; and that a more splendid light of the gospel has been kindled by the voice of Luther cannot be denied.

To that splendid list of most illustrious men raised up by God to gather and establish the Church, and recognised as the chief glory of the human race, must be added the name of Martin Luther. Solon, Themistocles, Scipio, Augustus and others who established or ruled over vast empires were great men indeed: but far inferior were they to our leaders, Isaiah, John the Baptist, Paul, Augustin and Luther. It is proper that we of the Church should understand this manifest difference.

What, then, are the great and splendid things disclosed by Luther which render his life illustrious? Many are crying out that confusion has come upon the Church, and that inexplicable controversies have arisen. I reply that this belongs to the regulation of the Church. When the Holy Spirit reproves the world, disorders arise on account of the obstinacy of the wicked. The fault is with those who will not hear the Son of God, of Whom the Heavenly Father says: "Hear ye him." Luther brought to light the true and necessary doctrine. That the densest darkness existed touching the doctrine of repentance is evident. In his discussions he showed what true repentance is, and what is the refuge and the sure comfort of the soul which quails under the sense of the wrath of God. He expounded Paul's doctrine, which says that man is justified by faith. He showed the difference between the law and the gospel, between the righteousness of faith and civil righteousness. He also showed what the true worship of God is: and [he] recalled the church from [the] heathenish superstition which imagined that God is worshipped, even though the mind, agitated by some academic doubt, turns away from God. He bade us worship in faith and with a good conscience, and led us to the one Mediator, the Son of God, who sits at the right hand of the Eternal Father and makes intercession for us—not to images or to dead men, that by a shocking superstition impious men might worship images and dead men.

He also pointed out other services acceptable to God, and so adorned and guarded civil life as it had never been adorned and guarded by any other man's writings. Then from necessary services he separated the puerilities of human ceremonies, the rites and institutions which hinder the true worship of God. And that the heavenly truth might be handed down to posterity he translated the prophetical and apostolic Scriptures into the German language with so much accuracy that his version is more easily understood by the reader than most commentaries.

He also published many expositions, which Erasmus was wont to say excelled all others. And as it is recorded respecting the rebuilding of Jerusalem that with one hand they builded and with the other they held the sword, so he fought with the enemies of the true doctrine, and at the same time composed annotations replete with heavenly truth, and by his pious counsel brought assistance to the consciences of many.

Inasmuch as a large part of the doctrine cannot be understood by human reason, as the doctrine of the remission of sins and of faith, it must be acknowledged that he was taught of God; and many of us witnessed the struggles through which he passed in establishing the principle that by faith are we received and heard of God.

Hence throughout eternity pious souls will magnify the benefits which God has bestowed on the Church through Luther. First they will give thanks to God. Then they will own that they owe much to the labors of this man, even though atheists who mock the Church declare that these splendid achievements are empty and superstitious nothings.

It is not true, as some falsely affirm, that intricate disputes have arisen, that the apple of discord has been thrown into the Church, that the riddles of the Sphinx have been proposed. It is an easy matter for discreet and pious persons, and for those who do not judge maliciously, to see, by a comparison of views, which [agree] with the heavenly doctrine and which do not. Yea, without doubt these controversies have already been settled in the minds of all pious persons. For since God wills to reveal himself and his purposes in the language of prophets and apostles, it is not to be imagined that that language is as ambiguous as the leaves of the Sibyl, which, when disturbed, fly away, the sport of the winds.

Some by no means evil-minded persons have complained that Luther displayed too much severity. I will not deny this. But I answer in the language of Erasmus: "Because of the magnitude of the disorders God gave this age a violent physician." When God raised up this instrument against the proud and impudent enemies of the truth, he spoke as he did to Jeremiah: "Behold I place my words in thy mouth; destroy and build." Over against these enemies God set this mighty destroyer. In vain do they find fault with God. Moreover, God does not govern the Church by human counsels; nor does He choose instruments very like those of men. It is natural for mediocre and inferior minds to dislike those of more ardent character, whether good or bad. When Aristides saw Themistocles by the mighty impulse of genius undertake and successfully accomplish great achievements, though he congratulated the State, he sought to turn the zealous mind of Themistocles from its course.

I do not deny that the more ardent characters sometimes make mistakes, for amid the weakness of human nature no one is without fault. But we may say of such a one what the ancients said of Hercules, Cimon and others: "rough indeed, but worthy of all praise." And in the Church, if, as Paul says, he wars a good warfare, holding faith and a good conscience, he is to be held in the highest esteem by us.

That Luther was such we do know, for he constantly defended purity of doctrine and kept a good conscience. There is no one who knew him who does not know that he was possessed of the greatest kindness and of the greatest affability in the society of his friends, and that he was in no sense contentious or quarrelsome. He also exhibited, as such a man ought, the greatest dignity of demeanor. He possessed "an upright character, a gracious speech."

Rather may we apply to him the words of Paul: "Whatsoever things are true, whatsoever things are honest, whatsoever things are just, whatsoever things are pure, whatsoever things are lovely, whatsoever things are of good report." If he was severe, it was the severity of zeal for the truth, not the love of strife or of harshness. Of these things we and many others are witnesses. To his sixty-third year he spent his life in the most ardent study of religion and of all the liberal arts. No speech of mine can worthily set forth the praises of such a man. No lewd passions were ever detected in him, no seditious counsels. He was emphatically the advocate of peace. He never mingled the arts of politics with the affairs of the Church for the purpose of augmenting his own authority or that of his friends. Such wisdom and virtue, I am persuaded, do not arise from mere human diligence. Brave, lofty, ardent souls, such as Luther had, must be divinely guided.

What shall I say of his other virtues? Often have I found him weeping and praying for the whole Church. He spent a part of almost every day reading the Psalms, with which he mingled his own supplications amid tears and groans. Often did he express his indignation at those who through indifference or pretence of other occupations are indifferent in the matter of prayer. On this account, he said, Divine Wisdom has prescribed forms of prayer, that by reading them our minds may be quickened, and the voice ever may proclaim the God we worship.

In the many grave deliberations incident to the public perils, we observed the transcendent vigor of his mind, his valor, his unshaken courage where terror reigned. God was his anchor, and faith never failed him.

As regards the penetration of his mind, in the midst of uncertainties he alone saw what was to be done. Nor was he indifferent, as many suppose, to the public weal. On the contrary he knew the wants of the state, and clearly understood the feelings and wishes of his fellow-citizens. And though his genius was so extraordinary, yet he read with the greatest eagerness both ancient and modern ecclesiastical writings and all histories, that he might find in them examples applicable to present conditions.

The immortal monuments of his eloquence remain, nor has the power of his oratory ever been surpassed.

The removal of such a man from our midst, a man of the most transcendent genius, skilled in learning, trained by long experience, adorned with many superb and heroic virtues, chosen of God for the reformation of the Church, loving us all with a paternal affection—the removal of such a man from our midst calls for tears and lamentations. We are like orphans bereft of a distinguished and faithful father. But though we must bow to God, yet let us not permit the memory of his virtues and of his good offices to perish from among us. And let us rejoice that he now holds that familiar and delightful intercourse with God and His Son, our Lord Jesus Christ, which by faith in the Son of God he always sought and expected. Where, by the manifestations of God and by the testimony of the whole Church in heaven, he not only hears the applause of his toils in the service of the gospel, but is also delivered from the mortal body as from a prison, and has entered that vastly higher school, where he can contemplate the essence of God, the two natures joined in Christ, and the whole purpose set forth in founding and redeeming the Church—which great things, contained and set forth in the sacred oracles, he contemplated by faith; but seeing them now face to face, he rejoices with unspeakable joy; and with his whole soul he ardently pours forth thanks to God for His great goodness.

There he knows why the Son of God is called the Word and the Image of the Eternal Father, and in what way the Holy Spirit is the bond of mutual affection, not only between the Father and Son, but also between them and the Church. The first principles of these truths he had learned in this mortal life, and often did he most earnestly and wisely discourse on these lofty themes, on the distinction between true and false worship, on the true knowledge of God and of divine revelation, on the true God as distinguished from false deities.

Many persons in this assembly have heard him discourse on these words: "Ye shall see the heaven open, and the angels of God ascending and descending upon the Son of man." He bade his hearers fix their minds on that large word of comfort which declares that heaven is open, that God is revealed to us; that the bolts of the divine wrath are turned away from those who flee to the Son; that God is now with us, and that those who call upon Him are received, guided and kept by him.

This purpose of God, pronounced by atheists to be a fable, admonishes us to banish doubt and to cast out those fears which restrain our timid souls from calling on God and from resting in Him.

He was wont to say that the angels, ascending and descending in the body of Christ, are ministers of the gospel, who first under the direction of Christ ascend to God and receive from Him the light of the gospel and the Holy Spirit. Then they descend, that is, discharge the office of teaching among men. He was also accustomed to add that these heavenly spirits, these angels who behold the Son, study and rejoice over the mysterious union of the two natures; and that since they are the armed servants of the Lord in defending the Church, they are directed by His hand.

Of these glorious things he is now a spectator, and as once under the direction of Christ he ascended and descended among the ministers of the gospel, so now he beholds the angels sent by Christ, and enjoys with them the contemplation of the divine wisdom and the divine works.

We remember the great delight with which he recounted the course, the counsels, the perils and escapes of the prophets, and the learning with which he discoursed on all the ages of the Church, thereby showing that he was inflamed by no ordinary passion for those wonderful men. Now he embraces them and rejoices to hear them speak, and to speak to them in turn. Now they hail him gladly as a companion, and thank God with him for having gathered and preserved the Church.

Hence we do not doubt that Luther is eternally happy. We mourn over our bereavement; and though it is necessary to bow to the will of God who has called him hence, let us know that it is the will of God that we should cherish the memory of this man's virtues and services. That duty let us now discharge. Let us acknowledge that this man was a blessed instrument of God, and let us studiously learn his doctrine. Let us in our humble station imitate his virtues, so necessary for us: his fear of God, his faith, his devoutness in prayer, his uprightness in the ministry, his chastity, his diligence in avoiding seditious counsels, his eagerness for learning. And as we ought frequently to reflect on those other pious leaders of the Church, Jeremiah, John the Baptist and Paul, so let us consider the doctrine and the course of this man. Let us also join in thanksgiving and prayer, as is meet in this assembly. Follow me then with devout hearts:—We give thanks to thee, Almighty God, the Eternal Father of our Lord Jesus Christ, the Founder of Thy Church, together with Thy Coeternal Son, and the Holy Spirit, wise, good, merciful, just, true, powerful Sovereign, because Thou dost gather a heritage for Thy Son from among the human race, and dost maintain the ministry of the gospel, and hast now reformed Thy Church by means of Luther. We present our ardent supplications that Thou wouldst henceforth preserve, fix and impress upon our hearts the doctrines of truth, as Isaiah prayed for his disciples; and that by Thy Holy Spirit Thou wouldst inflame our minds with a pure devotion and direct our feet into the paths of holy obedience.

As the death of illustrious rulers often portends dire punishment to the survivors, we beseech you, we, especially, to whom is committed the office of teaching, beseech you to reflect on the perils that now threaten the whole world. Yonder, the Turks are advancing; here, civil discord is threatened; there, other adversaries, released at last from the fear of Luther's censure, will corrupt the truth more boldly than ever.

That God may avert these calamities, let us be more diligent in regulating our lives and in directing our studies, always holding fast this sentiment: that so long as we retain, hear, learn and love the pure teaching of the gospel, we shall be the House and Church of God, as the Son of God says: "If a man love me, he will keep my words; and my Father will love him, and we will come unto him, and make our abode with him." Encouraged by this ample promise, let us be quickened in teaching the truth of heaven, and let us not forget that the human race and governments are preserved for the sake of the Church; and let us fix our eyes on that eternity to which God has called our attention, Who has not revealed Himself by such splendid witnesses and sent His Son in vain, but truly loves and cares for those who magnify His benefits. Amen.

Part Three

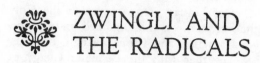

ZWINGLI AND
THE RADICALS

1. Zwingli: The First Zurich Disputation
and The Sixty-seven Articles

Ulrich Zwingli, the people's priest in the Great Minster in
Zurich, worked for a reform in the church initially guided by
Erasmian humanist impulses, but increasingly under evangelical influence. The Word of God as the purest authority
became for him the canon of all faith and life. Impressed by
the example of Luther's debate with the Catholic apologist
Dr. John Eck at Leipzig, Zwingli long cherished a plan for a
public discussion of religion which would clarify the points
at issue. Friends and foes, including the episcopal curia in
Constance, were invited to the Zurich town hall on January
29, 1523. Six hundred men assembled there, among them the
diocesan chancellor John Faber, the Vicar General. Zwingli
sat in the center at the front with his Hebrew, Greek, and
Latin Bibles open before him. He had prepared Sixty-Seven
Articles as a basis for the discussion. The first fifteen articles
state his positive doctrines, what the gospel is, who Christ is,
what the Church is. The remainder constitute his objections
to the pope, the mass, intercession of the saints, compulsory
fasting, pilgrimages, monastic vows, clerical celibacy, gabbled
prayers, indulgences, confessions, purgatory and other teachings and practices. The disputation resulted in enthusiastic
approval of Zwingli's teachings and an order from the authorities that all priests of the canton should promote them. From
Selected Works of Huldreich Zwingli (1484-1531), Samuel
Macauley Jackson, ed. (Philadelphia: University of Pennsylvania, 1901), pp. 40, 47-54, 111-117.

Acts of the Convention Held in the Praiseworthy City of Zurich on the 29th Day of January, On Account of the Holy Gospel—Being A Disputation Between the Dignified and Honorable Representative From Constance and Ulrich Zwingli, Preacher of the Gospel of Christ, Together with the Common Clergy of the Whole Territory of the Aforesaid City of Zurich, Held Before The Assembled Council in the Year 1523.

Master Ulrich Zwingli spoke . . . as follows:
Pious brothers in Christ, Almighty God has always shown His divine grace, will and favor to man from the beginning of the world, has been as kind as a true and almighty Father, as we read and know from all the Scriptures, so that everlasting, merciful God has communicated His divine Word and His will to man as a consolation. And although at some times He has kept away this same Word, the light of truth, from the sinful and godless struggling against the truth, and although He has allowed to fall into error those men who followed their own will and the leadings of their wicked nature, as we are truly informed in all Bible histories, still He has always in turn consoled His own people with the light of His everlasting Word; so that, whereas they had fallen into sin and error, they may again be lifted by His divine mercy; and He has never entirely forsaken them or let them depart from His divine recognition. This I say to you, dear brethren, for this purpose. You know that now in our time, as also many years heretofore, the pure, clear and bright light, the Word of God, has been so dimmed and confused and paled with human ambitions and teachings that the majority who by word of mouth call themselves Christians know nothing less well than the divine will. But by their own invented service of God, holiness, external spiritual exhibition, founded upon human customs and laws, they have gone astray, and have thus been persuaded by those whom people consider learned and leaders of others to the extent that the simple think that such invented external worship is spiritual, and that the worship of God, which they have put upon themselves, necessarily conduces to happiness. [But] all our true happiness, consolation and good consists, not in our merits, nor in such external works, [but] alone in Jesus Christ our Saviour, to whom the heavenly Father Himself gave witness that we should hear

Him as His beloved Son. His will and true service we can learn
and discover only from His true Word in the Holy Scriptures and
in the trustworthy writings of His twelve apostles, otherwise from
no human laws and statutes. Since now certain pious hearts have
ventured to preach this by the grace and inspiration of God's
holy spirit, and to bring it before the people, they call these
preachers not Christians but persecutors of the Christian Church
and even heretics. I am considered one of these by many of the
clergy and the laity everywhere in the Confederation. And although I know that for the past five years I have preached in this
city of Zurich nothing but the true, pure and clear Word of God,
the holy gospel, the joyous message of Christ, the Holy Scripture,
not by the aid of man but by the aid of the Holy Ghost, still all
this did not help me. But I am maligned by many as a heretic,
a liar, a deceiver and one disobedient to the Christian Church,
which facts are well known to my Lords of Zurich. I made complaint of these things before them as my lords; I have often entreated and begged of them in the public pulpit to grant me permission to give an account of my sermons and preachings (delivered in their city) before all men, learned or not, spiritual or
secular, also before our gracious Lord, the Bishop of Constance,
or his representative. This I also offered to do in the city of
Constance, providing a safe permit was assured me, as has ever
been done in the case of those from Constance. At such request of
mine, my lords, perhaps by divine will, you have granted me
permission to hold a discussion in German before the assembled
Council, for which privilege I thank you especially as my lords.
I have also brought together in outline the contents and import
of all my speeches and sermons delivered at Zurich, have issued
the same in German through the press, so that everyone might
see and know what my doctrine and sermons at Zurich have been
and shall be in the future, unless I am convinced of something
else. I hope and am confident, indeed I know, that my sermons and
doctrine are nothing else than the holy, true, pure gospel, which
God desired me to speak by the intuition and inspiration of His
spirit. But from what intent or desire God has wished such things
to take place through me, His unworthy servant, I cannot know,
for He alone knows and understands the secret of His counsels.
Wherefore I offer here to anyone who thinks that my sermons or

teachings are unchristian or heretical to give the reasons and to answer kindly and without anger. Now let them speak in the name of God. Here I am.

At such remarks of Master Ulrich the Vicar from Constance arose, and answered as follows:

Learned, worthy, noble, steadfast, favorable, wise, etc. My good fellow-brother and Lord, Master Ulrich, begins and complains that he has always preached the holy gospel here publicly in Zurich, of which I have no doubt, for who would not truly and faithfully preach the holy gospel and St. Paul, providing God had ordained him as a preacher? For I am also a preacher or priest, perhaps unworthy, but I have taught those entrusted to me for instruction in the Word of God in nothing but the true gospel, which I can also prove with true witness. And I shall for the future not in any way cease to preach this, providing God does not require me for other labors in the service of my gracious Lord of Constance. For the holy gospel is a power of God, as St. Paul writes to the Romans (i. 16), to each one who believes therein.

But now that Master Ulrich begins and complains that certain people blame him as not having spoken and preached the truth, but offers and has offered to answer for his speeches and sermons to any one, also (even) in Constance, I say, dear lords, that if Master Ulrich, my good lord and friend, should come to me in Constance I would show him as my good friend and lord all friendship and honor as far as lay in my power, and if he so desires would also entertain him in my house, not only as a good friend but also as a brother. Of this he is assured at my hands. Further, I say that I did not come here to oppose evangelical or apostolical doctrines, but to hear those who are said to speak or to have spoken against the doctrine of the holy gospel, and if any dissension should arise or should have arisen to help to judge and to decide the matter in kindness, as far as may be, to the end of peace and harmony rather than . . . discord. For the gospel and the divine Paul teach only what serves to grace and peace, not to disturbance and strife. But if there is a desire to dispute and oppose good old customs, the ways and usages of the past, then in such case I say that I shall not undertake to dispute anything here at Zurich. For, as I think, such matters are to be settled by a general Christian assembly of all nations, or by a council of bishops and other scholars as are found at universities, just as occurred in times past among the holy apostles in Jerusalem, as we read in Acts 15. For if such matters touching the common customs and the praiseworthy usages of the past were discussed and some decision reached˄ against them, such changes would perhaps not please other Christians dwelling in other places, who would doubtless assert that they had not consented to our views. For what would those in Spain, in Italy, in France and in the North say about it? Such things must surely, as I said, be ratified and maintained as formerly, by a general council, in order to be valid elsewhere. Therefore, dear lords, I speak now for myself. As a Christian member and brother in Christ I beg and urge you to consider these things well, lest hereafter further and greater strife and harm may result. Accordingly it would be my sincere advice to drop any difference or dissension that may have arisen concerning papal or other ecclesiastical ordinances (*constitutions*) of long standing, and without further disputing to lay aside and postpone them, to see if they could not be arranged meantime more peacefully and advantageously. For my gracious Lord of Constance is informed that it is decided at Nuremberg by the estates (*Ständen*) of the empire to hold a general council of the German nation within a year, in which I hear half the judges selected are secular and the other half ecclesiastical, and they are to judge and decide about the things which are now disturbing nearly all the world. If such takes place these matters should be referred to them as having the authority and power. And so it is the earnest desire of my lord, as far as possible, to have such differences about the clergy settled without dispute for the good of yourselves and all (other) Christians. For though these old ordinances, laws and customs should be discussed *pro* and *con* upon scriptural basis, who would be judge of these matters? According to my opinion whatever . . . one would discuss should be brought before the universities, as at Paris, Cologne or Louvain. (Here all laughed, for Zwingli interrupted by asking: "How about Erfurt? Would not Wittenberg do?" Then the legate said: "No; Luther was too near." He also said: "All bad things come from the North.") There one can find many taught in the Scriptures, who have ability to handle so great subjects. In this remark I do not wish to be taken as speaking to the discredit of any one's honor or knowledge, but as a Christian member, and with entire good nature I announce this. But as far as my office and commission are concerned, I have been sent here, as I said before, for no other purpose than to listen, and not to dispute.

Then Master Ulrich Zwingli spoke as follows: Pious brothers in Christ, the worthy Lord Vicar seeks so many evasions and subterfuges for the purpose of turning [you away] from . . . understanding with artful, rhetorical, evasive words. For he claims and says that he does not desire to discuss the good old customs or venerable usages concerning ecclesiastical ordinances, but I say that we do not want to ask here how long this or that custom or habit has been in use. But we desire to speak of the truth (to find out), whether a man is bound by divine ordinance to keep that which on account of long usage has been set up as law by men. For we of course think (as also the pope's own decree says) that custom should yield to truth. As to claiming that such matters should be settled by a Christian assembly of all nations, or by a council of bishops, etc., I say that here in this room is without doubt a Christian assembly. . . .

The Sixty-seven Articles of Zwingli

The articles and opinions below, I, Ulrich Zwingli, confess to have preached in the worthy city of Zurich as based upon the Scriptures which are called inspired by God, and I offer to protect and conquer with the said articles, and where I have not now correctly understood said Scriptures I shall allow myself to be taught better, but only from said Scriptures.

1. All who say that the gospel is invalid without the confirmation of the Church err and slander God.

2. The sum and substance of the gospel is that our Lord Jesus Christ, the true Son of God, has made known to us the will of His heavenly Father, and has with His innocence released us from death and reconciled God.

3. Hence Christ is the only way to salvation for all who ever were, are and shall be.

4. Who seeks or points out another door errs, yea, he is a murderer of souls and a thief.

5. Hence all who consider other teachings equal to or higher than the gospel err and do not know what the gospel is.

6. For Jesus Christ is the guide and leader, promised by God to all human beings, which promise was fulfilled.

7. . . . He is an eternal salvation and head of all believers, who are his body, but which is dead and can do nothing without him.

8. From this follows first that all who dwell in the Head are members and children of God, and that is the Church or communion of saints, the bride of Christ, *Ecclesia catholica*.

9. Furthermore, that as the members of the body can do nothing without the control of the head, so no one in the body of Christ can do the least without his head, Christ.

10. As that man is mad whose limbs [try to] do something without his head, tearing, wounding, injuring himself; thus when the members of Christ undertake something without their head, Christ, they are mad, and injure and burden themselves with unwise ordinances.

11. Hence we see in the clerical (so-called ordinances, concerning their splendor, riches, classes, titles, laws, a cause of all foolishness, for they do not also agree with the head.

12. Thus they still rage, not on account of the head (for that one is eager to bring forth in these times from the grace of God), but because one will not let them rage, but tries to compel them to listen to the head.

13. Where this (the head) is hearkened to one learns clearly and plainly the will of God, and man is attracted by His spirit to Him and changed into Him.

14. Therefore all Christian people shall use their best diligence that the gospel of Christ be preached alike everywhere.

15. For in the faith rests our salvation, and in unbelief our damnation; for all truth is clear in Him.

16. In the gospel one learns that human doctrines and decrees do not aid in salvation.

ABOUT THE POPE

17. That Christ is the only eternal high priest, wherefrom it follows that those who have called themselves high priests have opposed the honor and power of Christ, yea, cast it out.

ABOUT THE MASS

18. That Christ, having sacrificed Himself once, is to eternity a certain and valid sacrifice for the sins of all faithful, wherefrom it follows that the mass is not a sacrifice, but is a remembrance of the sacrifice and assurance of the salvation which God has given us.

19. That Christ is the only mediator between God and us.

ABOUT THE INTERCESSION OF SAINTS

20. That God desires to give us all things in His name, whence it follows that outside of this life we need no mediator except Himself.

21. That when we pray for each other on earth, we do so in such fashion that we believe that all things are given to us through Christ alone.

ABOUT GOOD WORKS

22. That Christ is our justice, from which [it] follows that our works insofar as they are good, so far they are of Christ, but insofar as they are ours, they are neither right nor good.

CONCERNING CLERICAL PROPERTY

23. That Christ scorns the property and pomp of this world, whence . . . it follows that those who attract wealth to themselves in His name slander Him terribly when they make Him a pretext for their avarice and wilfullness.

CONCERNING THE FORBIDDING OF FOOD

24. That no Christian is bound to do those things which God has not decreed, therefore one may eat at all times all food, wherefrom one learns that the decree about cheese and butter is a Roman swindle.

ABOUT HOLIDAY AND PILGRIMAGE

25. That time and place [are] under the jurisdiction of Christian people, and man with them, wherefrom is learned that those who fix time and place deprive the Christians of their liberty.

ABOUT HOODS, DRESS, INSIGNIA

26. That God is displeased with nothing so much as with hypocrisy; whence is learned that all is gross hypocrisy and profligacy which is mere show before men. Under this condemnation fall hoods, insignia, plates, etc.

ABOUT ORDERS AND SECTS

27. That all Christian men are brethren of Christ and brethren of one another, and shall create no father (for themselves) on earth. Under this condemnation fall orders, sects, brotherhoods, etc.

ABOUT THE MARRIAGE OF ECCLESIASTS

28. That all which God has allowed or not forbidden is righteous, hence marriage is permitted to all human beings.
29. That all who are called clericals sin when they do not protect themselves by marriage after they have become conscious that God has not enabled them to remain chaste.

ABOUT THE VOW OF CHASTITY

30. That those who promise chastity [outside of matrimony] take foolishly or childishly too much upon themselves, whence is learned that those who make such vows do wrong to the pious being.

ABOUT THE BAN

31. That no special person can impose the ban upon anyone, but [only] the Church, that is the congregation of those among

whom the one to be banned dwells, together with their watchman, i.e., the pastor.

32. That one may ban only him who gives public offence.

ABOUT ILLEGAL PROPERTY

33. That property unrighteously acquired shall not be given to temples, monasteries, cathedrals, clergy or nuns, but to the needy, if it cannot be returned to the legal owner.

ABOUT MAGISTRY

34. The spiritual (so-called) power has no justification for its pomp in the teaching of Christ.

35. But the lay has power and confirmation from the deed and doctrine of Christ.

36. All that the spiritual so-called state claims to have of power and protection belongs to the lay, if they wish to be Christians.

37. To them, furthermore, all Christians owe obedience without exception.

38. Insofar as they do not command that which is contrary to God.

39. Therefore all their laws shall be in harmony with the divine will, so that they protect the oppressed, even if he does not complain.

40. They alone may put to death justly, also, only those who give public offence (if God is not offended let another thing be commanded).

41. If they give good advice and help to those for whom they must account to God, then these owe to them bodily assistance.

42. But if they are unfaithful and transgress the laws of Christ they may be deposed in the name of God.

43. In short, the realm of him is best and most stable who rules in the name of God alone, and his is worst and most unstable who rules in accordance with his own will.

ABOUT PRAYER

44. Real petitioners call to God in spirit and truly, without great ado before men.

45. Hypocrites do their work so that they may be seen by men; [they] also receive their reward in this life.

46. Hence it must always follow that church song and outcry without devoutness and only for reward is seeking either fame before men or gain.

ABOUT OFFENCE

47. Bodily death a man should suffer before he offend or scandalize a Christian.

48. [A man] who through stupidness or ignorance is offended without cause . . . should not be left sick or weak, but . . . should be made strong, that he may not consider as a sin [that] which is not a sin.

49. Greater offence I know not than that one does not allow priests to have wives, but permits them to hire prostitutes. Out upon the shame!

ABOUT REMITTANCE OF SIN

50. God alone remits sin through Jesus Christ, His Son and alone our Lord.

51. [He] who assigns this to creatures detracts from the honor of God and gives it to him who is not God; this is real idolatry.

52. Hence the confession which is made to the priest or neighbor shall not be declared to be a remittance of sin, but only a seeking for advice.

53. Works of penance coming from the counsel of human beings (except the ban) do not cancel sin; they are imposed as a menace to others.

54. Christ has borne all our pains and labor. Hence whoever assigns to works of penance what belongs to Christ errs and slanders God.

55. Whoever pretends to remit to a penitent being any sin would not be a vicar of God or St. Peter, but of the devil.

56. Whoever remits any sin only for the sake of money is the companion of Simon and Balaam, and the real messenger of the devil personified.

ABOUT PURGATORY

57. The true divine Scriptures know naught about purgatory after this life.

58. The sentence of the dead is known to God only.

59. And the less God has let us know concerning it, the less we should undertake to know about it.

60. That man earnestly calls to God to show mercy to the dead I do not condemn, but to determine a period of time therefor (seven years for a mortal sin), and to lie for the sake of gain, is not human but devilish.

ABOUT THE PRIESTHOOD

61. About the consecration which the priests have received in late times the Scriptures know nothing.

62. Furthermore, they know no priests except those who proclaim the Word of God.

63. They command honor should be shown, i.e., to furnish them with food for the body.

ABOUT THE CESSATION OF MISUSAGES

64. All those who recognize their errors shall not be allowed to suffer but to die in peace, and thereafter arrange in a Christian manner their bequests to the Church.

65. Those who do not wish to confess, God will probably take care of. Hence no force shall be used against their body, unless it be that they behave so criminally that one cannot do without that.

66. All the clerical superiors shall at once settle down, and with unanimity set up the cross of Christ, not the money chests, or they will perish; for I tell thee the axe is raised against the tree.

67. If anyone wishes conversation with me concerning interest, tithes, unbaptized children or confirmation, I am willing to answer.

Let no one undertake here to argue with sophistry of human foolishness, but come to the Scriptures to accept them as the judge (*foras cares!* the Scriptures breathe the Spirit of God), so that the truth either may be found, or if found, as I hope, retained. Amen.

Thus may God rule.

2. Sattler: The Schleitheim Confession of Faith

The first Anabaptist community was a revival movement inspired by the preaching of Zwingli, much to his amazement and distress. He assaulted these radical reformers in sermons and in a special treatise *Against the Tricks of the Katabaptists* or rebaptizers, for he opposed their rejection of infant baptism, their negative attitude toward civil government and use of force, and believed reports of dissolute behavior and social disorder. A more positive picture of the Anabaptists is reflected in their oldest credal statement, *The Schleitheim Confession of Faith,* which was adopted at a conference of Swiss Brethren held on Saint Matthew's Day (February 24), 1527. It circulated widely and elicited refutations from Zwingli and many years later from Calvin. Michael Sattler (c. 1490-1527), the main author of this *Confession,* was a leader of Swiss and South German Anabaptism. In the *Confession* he did not attempt to cover the entire scope of Christian doctrine, but rather summarized the differences between the Swiss Brethren and the magisterial reformers. From John C. Wenger, "The Schleitheim Confession of Faith," *The Mennonite Quarterly Review,* XIX, No. 4 (October, 1945), 247-252. Reprinted by permission of the publishers.

Brotherly Union of a Number of Children of God Concerning Seven Articles

May joy, peace and mercy from our Father through the atonement of the blood of Christ Jesus, together with the gifts of the Spirit—Who is sent from the Father to all believers for their strength and comfort and for their perseverence in all tribulation until the end, Amen—be to all those who love God, who are the children of light, and who are scattered everywhere as it has been ordained of God our Father, where they are with one mind assembled together in one God and Father of us all: Grace and peace of heart be with you all, Amen.

Beloved brethren and sisters in the Lord: First and supremely we are always concerned for your consolation and the assurance of your conscience (which was previously misled) so that you may not always remain foreigners to us and by right almost completely excluded, but that you may turn again to the true implanted members of Christ, who have been armed through patience and knowledge of themselves, and have therefore again been united with us in the strength of a godly Christian spirit and zeal for God.

It is also apparent with what cunning the devil has turned us aside, so that he might destroy and bring to an end the work of God which in mercy and grace has been partly begun in us. But Christ, the true Shepherd of our souls, Who has begun this in us, will certainly direct the same and teach [us] to His honor and our salvation, Amen.

Dear brethren and sisters: we who have been assembled in the Lord at Schleitheim on the Border make known in points and articles to all who love God that as concerns us we are of one mind to abide in the Lord as God's obedient children, [His] sons and daughters, we who have been and shall be separated from the world in everything, [and] completely at peace. To God alone be praise and glory without the contradiction of any brethren. In this we have perceived the oneness of the Spirit of our Father and of our common Christ with us. For the Lord is the Lord of peace and not of quarreling, as Paul points out. That you may understand in what articles this has been formulated you should observe and note [the following].

A very great offense has been introduced by certain false brethren among us, so that some have turned aside from the faith, in the way they intend to practice and observe the freedom of the Spirit and of Christ. But such have missed the truth and to their con-demnation are given over to the lasciviousness and self-indulgence of the flesh. They think faith and love may do and permit every-thing, and nothing will harm them nor condemn them, since they are believers.

Observe, you who are God's members in Christ Jesus, that faith in the Heavenly Father through Jesus Christ does not take such form. It does not produce and result in such things as these false brethren and sisters do and teach. Guard yourselves and be warned of such people, for they do not serve our Father, but their father, the devil.

But you are not that way. For they that are Christ's have crucified the flesh with its passions and lusts. You understand me well and [know] the brethren whom we mean. Separate yourselves from them for they are perverted. Petition the Lord that they may have the knowledge which leads to repentance, and [pray] for us that we may have constancy to persevere in the way in which we have espoused, for the honor of God and of Christ, His Son, Amen.

The articles which we discussed and on which we were of one mind are these: 1. Baptism; 2. The Ban [Excommunication]; 3. Breaking of Bread; 4. Separation from the Abomination; 5. Pastors in the Church; 6. The Sword; and 7. The Oath.

First. Observe concerning baptism: Baptism shall be given to all those who have learned repentance and amendment of life and who believe truly that their sins are taken away by Christ; and to all those who walk in the resurrection of Jesus Christ and wish to be buried with Him in death, so that they may be resurrected with Him; and to all those who with this significance request it [baptism] of us and demand it for themselves. This excludes all infant baptism, the highest and chief abomination of the pope. In this you have the foundation and testimony of the apostles. Matt. 28, Mark 16, Acts 2, 8, 16, 19. This we wish to hold simply, yet firmly and with assurance.

Second. We are agreed as follows on the ban: The ban shall be employed with all those who have given themselves to the Lord, to walk in His commandments, and with all those who are baptized into the one body of Christ and who are called brethren or sisters, and yet who slip sometimes and fall into error and sin, being inadvertently overtaken. The same shall be admonished twice in secret and the third time openly disciplined or banned according to the command of Christ. Matt. 18. But this shall be done according to the regulation of the Spirit (Matt. 5) before the breaking of bread, so that we may break and eat one bread, with one mind and in one love, and may drink of one cup.

Third. In the breaking of bread we are of one mind and are agreed [as follows]: All those who wish to break one bread in remembrance of the broken body of Christ, and all who wish to drink of one drink as a remembrance of the shed blood of Christ, shall be united beforehand by baptism in one body of Christ which is the church of God and whose Head is Christ. For as Paul points out we cannot at the same time be partakers of the Lord's table and the table of devils; we cannot at the same time drink the cup of the Lord and the cup of the devil. That is, all those who have fellowship with the dead works of darkness have no part in the light. Therefore all who follow the devil and the world have no part with those who are called unto God out of the world. All who live in evil have no part in the good.

Therefore it is and must be [thus]: Whoever has not been called by one God to one faith, to one baptism, to one Spirit, to one body, with all the children of God's church, cannot be made [into] one bread with them, as indeed must be done if one is truly to break bread according to the command of Christ.

Fourth. We are agreed [as follows] on separation: A separation shall be made from the evil and from the wickedness which the devil planted in the world, in this manner: simply that we shall not have fellowship with them [the wicked] and not run with them in the multitude of their abominations. This is the way it is: Since all who do not walk in the obedience of faith, and have not united themselves with God so that they wish to do His will, are a great abomination before God, it is not possible for anything to grow or issue from them except abominable things. For truly all creatures are in but two classes, good and bad, believing and unbelieving, darkness and light, the world and those who [have come] out of the world, God's temple and idols, Christ and Belial; and none can have part with the other.

To us then the command of the Lord is clear when He calls upon us to be separate from the evil and thus He will be our God and we shall be His sons and daughters.

He further admonishes us to withdraw from Babylon and the earthly Egypt that we may not be partakers of the pain and suffering which the Lord will bring upon them.

From all this we should learn that everything which is not united with our God and Christ cannot be other than an abomination which we should shun and flee from. By this is meant all popish and antipopish works and church services, meetings and church attendance, drinking houses, civic affairs, the commitments [made in] unbelief and other things of that kind, which are highly regarded by the world and yet are carried on in flat contradiction to the command of God, in accordance with all the unrighteousness which is in the world. From all these things we shall be separated and have no part with them for they are nothing but an abomination, and they are the cause of our being hated before our Christ Jesus, Who has set us free from the slavery of the flesh and fitted us for the service of God through the Spirit Whom He has given us.

Therefore there will also unquestionably fall from us the unchristian, devilish weapons of force—such as sword, armor and the like, and all use [either] for friends or against one's enemies—by virtue of the word of Christ, "Resist not [him that is] evil."

Fifth. We are agreed as follows on pastors in the Church of God: The pastor in the Church of God shall, as Paul has prescribed, be one who out-and-out has a good report of those who are outside the faith. This office shall be to read, to admonish and teach, to warn, to discipline, to ban in the church, to lead out in prayer for the advancement of all the brethren and sisters, to lift up the bread when it is to be broken, and in all things to see to the care of the body of Christ, in order that it may be built up and developed, and the mouth of the slanderer be stopped.

This one moreover shall be supported [by] the church which has chosen him, wherein he may be in need, so that he who serves the gospel may live of the gospel as the Lord has ordained. But if a pastor should do something requiring discipline, he shall not be dealt with except [on the testimony of] two or three witnesses. And when they sin they shall be disciplined before all in order that the others may fear.

But should it happen that through the cross this pastor should be banished or led to the Lord [through martyrdom] another shall be ordained in his place in the same hour so that God's little flock and people may not be destroyed.

Sixth. We are agreed as follows concerning the sword: The sword is ordained of God outside the perfection of Christ. It punishes and puts to death the wicked, and guards and protects the good. In the law the sword was ordained for the punishment of the wicked and for their death, and the same [sword] is [now] ordained to be used by the worldly magistrates.

In the perfection of Christ, however, only the ban is used for a warning and for the excommunication of the one who has sinned, without putting the flesh to death—simply the warning and the command to sin no more.

Now it will be asked by many who do not recognize [this as] the will of Christ for us, whether a Christian may or should employ the sword against the wicked for the defense and protection of the good, or for the sake of love.

Our reply is unanimously as follows: Christ teaches and commands us to learn of Him, for He is meek and lowly in heart and so shall we find rest to our souls. Also Christ says to the heathenish woman who was taken in adultery, not that [she should be stoned] according to the law of His Father (and yet He says, "As the Father has commanded me, thus I do"), but in mercy and forgiveness and warning, to sin no more. Such [an attitude] we also ought to take completely according to the rule of the ban.

Secondly, it will be asked concerning the sword, whether a Christian shall pass sentence in worldly dispute and strife such as unbelievers have with one another. This is our united answer: Christ did not wish to decide or pass judgment between brother and brother in the case of the inheritance, but refused to do so. Therefore we should do likewise.

Thirdly, it will be asked concerning the sword, [whether] one [shall] be a magistrate if one should be chosen as such. The answer is as follows: They wished to make Christ king, but He fled and did not view it as the arrangement of His Father. Thus shall we do as He did, and follow Him, and so shall we not walk in darkness. For He Himself says, "He who wishes to come after me, let him deny himself and take up his cross and follow me." Also, He Himself forbids the [employment of] the force of the sword saying that the worldly princes lord it over them, etc., but not so shall it be with you. Further, Paul says, Whom God did foreknow He also did predestinate to be conformed to the image of His Son, etc. Also Peter says, Christ has suffered (not ruled) and left us an example, that [we] should follow His steps.

Finally it will be observed that it is not appropriate for a Christian to serve as a magistrate because of these points: The government magistracy is according to the flesh, but the Christians' is according to the Spirit. Their houses and dwelling remain in this world, but the Christians' are in heaven; their citizenship is in this world, but the Christians' citizenship is in heaven; the weapons of their conflict and war are carnal and against the flesh only, but the Christians' weapons are spiritual, against the fortifications of the devil. The worldlings are armed with steel and iron, but the Christians are armed with the armor of God, with truth, righteousness, peace, faith, salvation and the Word of God. In brief, as is the mind of Christ toward us, so shall the mind of the members of the body of Christ be through Him in all things, that there may be no schism in the body through which it would be destroyed. For every kingdom divided against itself will be destroyed. Now since Christ is as it is written of Him, His members must also be the same, that His body may remain complete and united to its own advancement and upbuilding.

Seventh. We are agreed as follows concerning the oath: The oath is a confirmation among those who are quarreling or making promises. In the law it is commanded to be performed in God's Name, but only in truth, not falsely. Christ, who teaches the perfection of the law, prohibits all swearing to His [followers], whether true or false—neither by heaven, nor by the earth, nor by Jerusalem, nor by our head— . . . for the reason which He shortly thereafter gives: For you are not able to make one hair white or black. So you see it is for this reason that all swearing is forbidden: we cannot fulfill that which we promise when we swear, for we cannot change [even] the very least thing on us.

Now there are some who do not give credence to the simple command of God, but object with this question: Well now, did not God swear to Abraham by Himself (since He was God) when He promised him that He would be with him and that He would be his God if he would keep His commandments? Why then should I not also swear when I promise to someone? Answer: Hear what the Scripture says: God, since He wished more abundantly to show unto the heirs the immutability of His counsel, inserted an oath, that by two immutable things (in which it is impossible for God to lie) we might have a strong consolation. Observe the meaning of this Scripture: What God forbids you to do, He has power to do, for everything is possible for Him. God swore an oath to Abraham, says the Scripture, so that He might show that His counsel is immutable. That is, no one can withstand nor thwart His will; therefore He can keep His oath. But we can do

nothing, as is said about by Christ, to keep or perform [our oaths];
therefore we shall not swear at all [*nichts schweren*].

Then others further say as follows: It is not forbidden of God
to swear in the New Testament, when it is actually commanded
in the Old, but it is forbidden only to swear by heaven, earth,
Jerusalem and our head. Answer: Hear the Scripture: He who
swears by heaven swears by God's throne and by Him who sitteth
thereon. Observe: it is forbidden to swear by heaven, which is
only the throne of God. How much more is it forbidden [to swear]
by God Himself! Ye fools and blind, which is greater, the throne
or Him that sitteth thereon?

Further some say: Because evil is now [in the world, and] because man needs God for [the establishment of] the truth, so did
the apostles Peter and Paul also swear. Answer: Peter and Paul
only testify of that which God promised to Abraham with the
oath. They themselves promised nothing, as the example indicates
clearly. Testifying and swearing are two different things. For when
a person swears he is in the first place promising future things,
as Christ was promised to Abraham Whom we a long time afterwards received. But when a person bears testimony he is testifying
about the present, whether it is good or evil, as Simeon spoke to
Mary about Christ and testified: Behold this (child) is set for the
fall and rising of many in Israel, and for a sign which shall be
spoken against.

Christ also taught us along the same line when He said, "Let
your communication be Yea, yea; Nay, nay; for whatsoever is more
than these cometh of evil." He says, Your speech or word shall be
yea and nay. (However) when one does not wish to understand,
he remains closed to the meaning. Christ is simply Yea and Nay,
and all those who seek Him simply will understand His Word.
Amen.

3. The Trial and Martyrdom of Michael Sattler
from Martyr's Mirror
Rottenburg, 1527

The saintly Anabaptist leader Michael Sattler was perhaps typical of the general membership in the movement by not being a prominent personage. Converted by evangelical preaching, he gave up his position as prior of St. Peter's in Breisgau and went to Zurich where he soon joined the Swiss Anabaptist Brethren. Exiled from Zurich he took refuge in more tolerant Strassburg and then moved to Horb in Wuerttemberg to do mission work for his cause. Shortly after he presided at the Anabaptist Schleitheim Conference in 1527, he was arrested by the Austrian authorities, tried and burned to death as a seditious person and heretic. The following account comes from Tilman J. van Braght's *Martyr's Mirror* (1660) which was based on earlier records. From *Spiritual and Anabaptist Writers* (Volume XXV: The Library of Christian Classics), edited by George Huston Williams and Angel M. Mergal. First published MCMLVII by SCM Press Ltd., London and The Westminster Press, Philadelphia. Used by permission of Westminster/John Knox Press.

After many legal transactions on the day of his departure from this world, the articles against him being many, Michael Sattler . . . requested that they might once more be read to him and that he might again be heard upon them. This the bailiff, as the attorney [for the defense] of his lord [the emperor], opposed and would not consent to. . . . Michael Sattler then requested a ruling. After a consultation, the judges returned as their answer that, if his opponents would allow it, they, the judges, would consent. Thereupon the town clerk of Ensisheim, as the spokesman of the said attorney, spoke thus: "Prudent, honorable

97

and wise lords, he has boasted of the Holy Ghost. Now if his boast is true, it seems to me, it is unnecessary to grant him this; for, if he has the Holy Ghost, as he boasts, the same will tell him what has been done here." To this Michael Sattler replied: "You servants of God, I hope my request will not be denied, for the said articles are as yet unclear to me [because of their number]." The town clerk responded: "Prudent, honorable and wise lords, though we are not bound to do this, yet in order to give satisfaction, we will grant him his request that it may not be thought that injustice is being done him in his heresy or that we desire to abridge him of his rights. Hence let the articles be read to him again." [The nine charges, seven against all fourteen defendants, two specifically against Sattler, are here omitted, as they are answered seriatim by Sattler.]

Thereupon Michael Sattler requested permission to confer with his brethren and sisters, which was granted him. Having conferred with them for a little while, he began and undauntedly answered as follows: "In regard to the articles relating to me and my brethren and sisters, hear this brief answer:

"First, that we have acted contrary to the imperial mandate, we do not admit. For the same says that the Lutheran doctrine and delusion is not to be adhered to, but only the gospel and the Word of God. This we have kept. For I am not aware that we have acted contrary to the gospel and the Word of God. I appeal to the words of Christ.

"Secondly, that the real body of Christ the Lord is not present in the sacrament, we admit. For the Scripture says: Christ ascended into heaven and sitteth on the right hand of His Heavenly Father, whence He shall come to judge the quick and the dead, from which it follows that, if He is in heaven and not in the bread, He may not be eaten bodily.

"Thirdly, as to baptism we say infant baptism is of no avail to salvation. For it is written [Rom. 1:17] that we live by faith alone. Again [Mark 16:16]: 'He that believeth and is baptized shall be saved.' Peter says the same [I, 3:21]: 'Which doth also now save you in baptism (which is signified by that [Ark of Noah]), not the putting away of the filth of the flesh but rather the covenant of a good conscience with God by the resurrection of Jesus Christ.'

"Fourthly, we have not rejected the oil [of extreme unction]. For it is a creature of God, and what God has made is good and not to be refused; but that the pope, bishops, monks and priests can make it better we do not believe; for the pope never made anything good. That of which the Epistle of James [5:14] speaks is not the pope's oil.

"Fifthly, we have not insulted the mother of God and the saints. For the mother of Christ is to be blessed among all women because unto her was accorded the favor of giving birth to the Saviour of the whole world. But that she is a mediatrix and advocatess—of this the Scriptures know nothing, for she must with us await the judgment. Paul said to Timothy [I, 2:5]: Christ is our mediator and advocate with God. As regards the saints, we say that *we* who live and believe are the saints, which I prove by the epistles of Paul to the Romans [1:7], the Corinthians [I, 1:2], the Ephesians [1:1], and other places where he always writes 'to the beloved *saints*.' Hence, we who believe are the saints, but those who have died in the faith we regard as the blessed.

"Sixthly, we hold that we are not to swear before the authorities, for the Lord says [Matt. 5:34]: Swear not, but let your communication be, Yea, yea; nay, nay.

"Seventhly, when God called me to testify of his Word and I had read Paul and also considered the unchristian and perilous state in which I was, beholding the pomp, pride, usury and great whoredom of the monks and priests, I went and took unto me a wife, according to the command of God; for Paul well prophesies concerning this to Timothy [I, 4:3]: In the latter time it shall come to pass that men shall forbid to marry and command to abstain from meats which God hath created to be received with thanksgiving.

"Eighthly, if the Turks come, we ought not to resist them. For it is written [Matt. 5:21]: Thou shalt not kill. We must not defend ourselves against the Turks and others of our persecutors, but are to beseech God with earnest prayer to repel and resist them. But that I said that, if warring *were* right, I would rather take the field against so-called Christians who persecute, capture and kill pious Christians than against the Turks was for the following reason. The Turk is a true Turk, knows nothing of the Christian faith and is a Turk after the flesh. But you who would be Christians and who make your boast of Christ persecute the pious witnesses of Christ and are Turks after the spirit!

"In conclusion, ministers of God, I admonish you to consider the end for which God has appointed you, to punish the evil and to defend and protect the pious. Whereas, then, we have not acted contrary to God and the gospel, you will find that neither I nor my brethren and sisters have offended in word or deed against any authority. Therefore, ministers of God, if you have neither heard nor read the Word of God, send for the most learned men and for the sacred books of the Bible in whatsoever language they may be and let them confer with us in the Word of God. If they prove to us with the Holy Scriptures that we err and are in the wrong, we will gladly desist and recant and also willingly suffer the sentence and punishment for that of which we have been accused; but if no error is proven to us, I hope to God that you will be converted and receive instruction."

Upon this speech the judges laughed and put their heads together, and the town clerk of Ensisheim said: "Yes, you infamous, desperate rascal of a monk, should we dispute with you? The hangman will dispute with you, I assure you!"

Michael said: "God's will be done."

The town clerk said: "It were well if you had never been born."

Michael replied: "God knows what is good."

The town clerk: "You archheretic, you have seduced pious people. If they would only now forsake their error and commit themselves to grace!"

Michael: "Grace is with God alone."

One of the prisoners also said: "We must not depart from the truth."

The town clerk: "Yes, you desperate villain, you archheretic, I say, if there were no hangman here, I would hang you myself and be doing God a good service thereby."

Michael: "God will judge aright." Thereupon the town clerk said a few words to him in Latin, what, we do not know. Michael Sattler answered him, "*Judica.*"

The town clerk then admonished the judges and said: "He will not cease from this chatter anyway. Therefore, my Lord Judge, you may proceed with the sentence. I call for a decision of the court."

The judge asked Michael Sattler whether he too committed it to the court. He replied: "Ministers of God, I am not sent to judge the Word of God. We are sent to testify and hence cannot consent to any adjudication, since we have no command from God concerning it. But we are not for that reason removed from being judged and we are ready to suffer and to await what God is planning to do with us. We will continue in our faith in Christ so long as we have breath in us, unless we be dissuaded from it by the Scriptures."

The town clerk said: "The hangman will instruct you, he will dispute with you, archheretic."

Michael: "I appeal to the Scriptures."

Then the judges arose and went into another room where they remained for an hour and a half and determined on the sentence. In the meantime some of the soldiers in the room treated Michael Sattler most unmercifully, heaping reproach upon him. One of them said: "What have you in prospect for yourself and the others that you have so seduced them?" With this he also drew a sword which lay upon the table, saying: "See with this they will dispute with you." But Michael did not answer upon a single word concerning himself but willingly endured it all. One of the prisoners said: "We must not cast pearls before swine." Being also asked why he had not remained a lord in the convent, Michael answered: "According to the flesh I was a lord, but it is better as it is." He did not say more than what is recorded here, and this he spoke fearlessly.

The judges having returned to the room, the sentence was read. It was as follows: "In the case of the attorney of His Imperial Majesty vs. Michael Sattler, judgment is passed that Michael Sattler shall be delivered to the executioner, who shall lead him to the place of execution and cut out his tongue, then forge him fast to a wagon and thereon with red-hot tongs twice tear pieces from his body; and after he has been brought outside the gate, he shall be plied five times more in the same manner . . ."

After this had been done in the manner prescribed, he was burned to ashes as a heretic. His fellow brethren were executed with the sword, and the sisters drowned. His wife, also after being subjected to many entreaties, admonitions and threats, under which she remained steadfast, was drowned a few days afterward. Done the 21st day of May, A.D. 1527.

4. Servetus: On the Errors of the Trinity

During his law studies at Toulouse the young Spaniard Michael Servetus (1511-1553) had a moving religious experience in discovering in the Scriptures the historical person of Jesus of Nazareth, the Christ, who became the object and center of his faith. He turned against the traditional formulations of the nature of Christ and the relation of the persons of the Trinity. He believed that such terms as hypostases or persons, substance, essence, and the like were imposed upon Biblical conceptions from Greek metaphysics and as such were abstract, speculative, artificial, and unrelated to the living God. Having failed to convince the reformers in Basel and Strassburg of the propriety of his views, Servetus in 1531 published his treatise *On the Errors of the Trinity*. In so doing he left the impression that he was reviving the ancient Arian heresy that Jesus was not the preexistent Word who was with God the Father from eternity. His subsequent apology and his larger work on the *Restoration of Christianity* did not improve his reputation for orthodoxy. He was condemned on all sides and was recognized, tried, and burned at the stake in Geneva in 1553, a victim of a misguided zeal for truth on the part of Calvin and his followers, who acted even out of a concern for the man himself. The first paragraphs of the treatise *On the Errors of the Trinity* suggest the tone and general argument of the work. From Michael Servetus, *The Two Treatises of Servetus on the Trinity, Harvard Theological Studies*, XVI (Cambridge, Mass.: Harvard University Press, 1932), pp. 6-10. Reprinted by permission of the publishers.

In investigating the holy mysteries of the divine Triad, I have thought that one ought to start from the man; for I see most men approaching their lofty speculation about the Word without having any fundamental understanding of Christ, and they attach little or no importance to the man, and give the true Christ quite over to oblivion. But I shall endeavor to recall to their memories who the Christ is. However, what and how much importance is to be attached to Christ, the Church shall decide.

Seeing that the pronoun [*the* Christ] indicates a man, whom they call the human nature, I shall admit these three things: first, this man is Jesus Christ, second, he is the Son of God; third, he is God.

That he was called *Jesus* at the beginning, who would deny? That is, in accordance with the angel's command, the boy was on the day of his circumcision given a name, even as you were called John, and this man, Peter. Jesus, as Tertullian [a Latin church father] says, is a man's proper name, and Christ is a surname. The Jews all admitted that he was *Jesus*, but denied that he was *Christ*, asking about Jesus *who is called* Christ, and they put out of the synagogue those who confessed that he was Christ; and the Apostles had frequent disputes with them about him, as to whether Jesus were the Christ. But as to Jesus, there was never any doubt or question, nor did any one ever deny this name. See what the discourse is aiming at, and with what purpose Paul testifies to the Jews that Jesus is the Christ; with what fervor of spirit Apollos of Alexandria publicly confuted the Jews, showing by the Scriptures that Jesus was the Messiah. Of what Jesus do you suppose those things were said? Do you think they disputed there about a *hypostasis* [person]? I am bound therefore to admit that he was Christ as well as Jesus, since I admit that he was anointed of God; for this is *thy Holy Servant, whom thou didst anoint*. This is *the most holy*, who, [the Hebrew prophet] Daniel foretold, should be anointed. And [the Apostle] Peter spoke of it as an accomplished fact: Ye yourselves know, for the saying about Jesus is known to all men, namely, that God anointed Jesus of Nazareth with the Holy Spirit and with power, for God was with Him; and, *This is He who is ordained of God to be the Judge of the living and the dead;* and, *Let all the house of Israel know assuredly, that this Jesus whom ye crucified God hath made both Lord and Christ,* that is, anointed. Some, however, try to show that these pronouns mean another being. But John calls him a liar that denies that this Jesus is anointed of God; and, He that admits that Jesus is the Christ is begotten of God.

Tertullian also says that the term Christ is a word belonging to a human nature. And although he makes careful inquiry concerning the word Christ, he makes no mention of that being which some make Christ out to be. Who, he also says, is the Son of man, if not himself a man, born of a man, a body born of a body? For the Hebrew expression son of man, son of Adam, means nothing else than *man*. Again, the way the word is used implies this, for to be anointed can refer only to a human nature. If, then, being anointed, as he says, is an affair of the body, who can deny that the one anointed is a man? Moreover, in the Clementine Recognitions [Greek patristic writings] Peter brings out the meaning of the word: because kings used to be called Christs, therefore He, being distinguished above others by His anointing, is called Christ the king; because just as God made an angel chief over the angels, and a beast over the beasts, and a heavenly body over the heavenly bodies, so he made the man Christ chief over men.

Again, on the authority of Holy Scripture we are taught very plainly that Christ is called a man, since even an earthly king is called Christ. Again, *Of whom was born Jesus, the one who is called [the] Christ.* Note the article, and note the surname; for these words and the pronouns are to be understood in the simplest sense: they denote something perceived by the senses. Again, *Thou shalt call his name Jesus* [Luke 1, 31]; and he is very evidently writing of Jesus as a man, when he says, *And Jesus himself began to be thirty years of age, and was supposed to be the son of Joseph* [Luke 3, 23]. And, *Of David's seed hath God according to promise brought Jesus* [Acts 13, 23]. And John [the Baptist] said, "Think not that I am Christ." How absurd John's disclaimer would be, if the word Christ can not refer to a man. Moreover, to what end does Christ warn us to shun those men that called themselves Christs? Christ's question and Peter's answer would be silly, when Christ said, *Who do men say that I, the Son of man, am? And Peter answered, Thou art the Christ, thou art the Son of the living God.* Nor would it mean the living Word of God, for in speaking to a man he ought to have said, Christ is in thee, the Son of God is in thee, and not, Thou art. And when he charged them there that they should tell no man that he was Christ, tell me, what did he mean by that pronoun? For it is clearer than day that he meant himself, and was speaking of himself. Do you not blush to say that he was without a name, and that the Apostles had preached him so long [a] time without having called him by his own name; and do you on your own authority impose upon him a new and unfitting name, and one unheard of by the Apostles, calling him only the human nature?

Again, let not the Greek title [Christos] deceive you; but take the word [Messiah] or the Latin word *unctus*, and see whether you, who admit that we have been anointed, will venture to admit that he was anointed. Nor should I so strongly insist upon proving this point, which is clear enough at the very outset, were it not that I see that the minds of some are misled. Again, Christ's testimony is very clear, when he calls himself a man: *Ye seek to kill me, a man that hath told you the truth* [John 8, 40]. And, *A mediator between God and men, the man Christ Jesus* [1 Tim. 2:5]. Again, pay no regard to the word *homo*, which, if you hold to the *communicatio idiomatum*, has been corrupted in meaning; but take the word *vir* [man], and hear Peter when he says that Christ was *a man approved*. And, *Concerning Jesus the Nazarene, who was a man, a mighty prophet*. And, *After me cometh a man;* and, *Rejected of men, a man of sorrows;* and, *Behold, the man, whose name is the Branch;* and, *God will judge by that man,* namely, Christ.

Again, do not misrepresent the law of God by circumlocutions. Consider rather the nature of the demonstrative pronoun, and you will see that this is the original meaning of the word; for when he is pointed out to the eye it is very often admitted, This is the Christ, Thou art Jesus; and that he speaks, asks, answers, eats, and that they saw him walking upon the water. Likewise, I am he whom ye seek, Jesus of Nazareth; and *Whomsoever I shall kiss, that is he: take him.* And in another place, *It is I myself: handle me, and see;* and, *This Jesus, whom ye slew, did God raise up, whereof we all are witnesses.* Just what will you mean by such pronouns? As for an eye-witness, are we not in worse case than the Samaritan woman who said, *Come and see a man, who told me all things that ever I did: can this be the Christ?* No wonder that a woman founded on Christ spoke thus, for when she was herself looking for a Messiah to come, who is called Christ, he replied, *I that speak unto thee am he*—I, I, not the *being,* but, *I that speak.*

Again, to what man do you understand that that word of the Apostle refers, *As by the trespass of one man, . . . so by the grace of one man Jesus Christ;* and, *As by a man came death, so by a man came the resurrection of the dead?* For the Scripture does not take *man* connotatively; it calls him not only man, but Adam. Yet for our basis we would have a connotative man, and a speculative substance. Away, I pray, with these sophistical tricks, and you shall see a great light. The foundation of the Church is the words of Christ, which are most simple and plain. Let us imitate the

Apostles, who preached Christ not with words composed by art of man. The words of the Lord are pure words, they are to be received with simplicity. And witness the Apostle: *Not with excellency of speech* is the testimony of Christ to be proclaimed, but plainly, and as if we had become babes, and as if we knew nothing else *save* Jesus Christ, *and him crucified*.

5. Castellio: Concerning Heretics

Among the few truly liberal voices heard during the sixteenth century in favor of religious toleration was that of Sebastian Castellio (d. 1563), author of the work, *Concerning Heretics Whether They Are to Be Persecuted and How They Are to Be Treated.* Castellio, a native of Savoy, came to Geneva as a refugee from the Inquisition. He became a teacher there but was rejected for ordination because of non-conformist views. He then became a professor of Greek at the University of Basel, anticipating a quiet life of study. But the execution of Michael Servetus in Geneva in 1553 involved him in a bitter controversy and he was finally brought to trial himself for heresies, but died during the proceedings in 1563. In the Preface to *Concerning Heretics* addressed to the evangelical Prince Christoph of Wuerttemberg, presented here in part, he presented a parable to illustrate that tolerance and mutual love constitute a Christian imperative. From Sebastian Costellio, *Concerning Heretics Whether They Are to Be Persecuted and How They Are to Be Treated.* Roland H. Bainton, ed., (New York: Columbia University Press, 1935), pp. 121-123. Reprinted by permission of the publishers. Copyright © 1935.

Most Illustrious Prince, suppose you had told your subjects that you would come to them at some uncertain time and had commanded them to make ready to go forth clad in white garments to meet you whenever you might appear. What would you do if, on your return, you discovered that they had taken no thought for the white robes but instead were disputing among themselves concerning your person? Some were saying that you were in France, others that you were in Spain; some that you would come on a horse, others in a chariot; some were asserting that you would appear with a great equipage, others that you would be unattended. Would this please you?

Suppose further that the controversy was being conducted not merely by words but by blows and swords, and that one group wounded and killed the others who did not agree with them. "He will come on a horse," one would say.

"No, in a chariot," another would retort.

"You lie."

"You're the liar. Take that." He punches him.

"And take that in the belly." The other stabs.

Would you, O Prince, commend such citizens? Suppose, however, that some did their duty and followed your command to prepare the white robes, but the others oppressed them on that account and put them to death. Would you not rigorously destroy such scoundrels?

But what if these homicides claimed to have done all this in your name and in accord with your command, even though you had previously expressly forbidden it? Would you not consider that such outrageous conduct deserved to be punished without mercy? Now I beg you, most Illustrious Prince, to be kind enough to hear why I say these things.

Christ is the Prince of this world who on His departure from the earth foretold to men that He would return some day at an uncertain hour, and He commanded them to prepare white robes for His coming; that is to say, that they should live together in a Christian manner, amicably, without controversy and contention, loving one another. But consider now, I beg you, how well we discharge our duty.

How many are there who show the slightest concern to prepare the white robe? Who is there who bends every effort to live in this world in a saintly, just and religious manner in the expectation of the coming of the Lord? For nothing is there so little concern. The true fear of God and charity are fallen and grown cold. Our life is spent in contention and in every manner of sin. We dispute, not as to the way by which we may come to Christ, which is to correct our lives, but rather as to the state and office of Christ, where He now is and what He is doing, how He is seated at the right hand of the Father, and how He is one with the Father; likewise with regard to the Trinity, predestination, free will; so also of God, the angels, the state of souls after this life and other like things, which do not need to be known for salvation by faith (for the publicans and sinners were saved without this knowledge), nor indeed can they be known before the heart is pure (for to see these things is to see God Himself, who cannot be seen save by the pure in heart, as the text says, "Blessed are the pure in heart, for they shall see God"). Nor if these are known do they make a man better, as Paul says, "Though I understand all mysteries and have not love it profiteth me nothing." This perverse curiosity engenders worse evils. Men are puffed up with knowledge or with a false opinion of knowledge and look down upon others. Pride is followed by cruelty and persecution so that now scarcely anyone is able to endure another who differs at all from him. Although opinions are almost as numerous as men, nevertheless there is hardly any sect which does not condemn all others and desire to reign alone. Hence arise banishments, chains, imprisonments, stakes and gallows and this miserable rage to visit daily penalties upon those who differ from the mighty about matters hitherto unknown, for so many centuries disputed, and not yet cleared up.

If, however, there is someone who strives to prepare the white robe, that is, to live justly and innocently, then all others with one accord cry out against him if he differ from them in anything, and they confidently pronounce him a heretic on the ground that he seeks to be justified by works. Horrible crimes of which he never dreamed are attributed to him and the common people are prejudiced by slander until they consider it a crime merely to hear him speak. Hence arises such cruel rage that some are so incensed by calumny as to be infuriated when the victim is first strangled instead of being burned alive at a slow fire.

This is cruel enough, but a more capital offense is added when this conduct is justified under the robe of Christ and is defended as being in accord with His will, when Satan could not devise anything more repugnant to the nature and will of Christ! Yet these very people, who are so furious against the heretics, as they call them, are so far from hating moral offenders that no scruple is felt against living in luxury with the avaricious, currying flatterers, abetting the envious and calumniators, making merry with drunkards, gluttons and adulterers, banqueting daily with the scurrilous, imposters and those who are hated of God. Who then can doubt that they hate not vices but virtues? To hate the good is the same as to love the evil. If, then, the bad are dear to a man there is no doubt but that the good are hateful to him.

I ask you, then, most Illustrious Prince, what do you think Christ will do when He comes? Will He commend such things? Will He approve of them?

Part Four

CALVIN'S ECCLESIASTICAL REFORM

1. Calvin: Conversion and Call to Geneva

The great reformer John Calvin was less open and articulate about his own personal spiritual development than was Luther, who wore his heart on his sleeve. This very reticence about speaking of himself makes all the more precious the account of his own conversion and call to Geneva which he included almost incidentally in the Author's Preface to his *Commentary on the Book of Psalms*, dated July 22, 1557. From John Calvin, *Commentary on the Book of Psalms*, I. (Grand Rapids, Michigan: Wm. B. Eerdmans Publishing Company, 1949), xl-xliv. Used by permission of the publishers.

[Just] as he [King David] was taken from the sheepfold and elevated to the rank of supreme authority, so God having taken me from my originally obscure and humble condition has reckoned me worthy of being invested with the honorable office of a preacher and minister of the gospel. When I was as yet a very little boy, my father had destined me for the study of theology. But afterwards, when he considered that the legal profession commonly raised those who followed it to wealth, this prospect induced him suddenly to change his purpose. Thus it came to pass that I was withdrawn from the study of philosophy and was put to the study of law. To this pursuit I endeavored faithfully to apply myself, in obedience to the will of my father; but God, by the secret guidance of His providence, at length gave a different direction to my course. And first, since I was too obstinately devoted to the superstitions of popery to be easily extricated from so profound an abyss of mire, God by a sudden conversion subdued and brought my mind to a teachable frame, which was more hardened in such matters than might have been expected from one at my early period of life. Having thus received some taste and knowledge of true godliness, I was immediately inflamed with so intense a desire to make progress therein, that although I did not altogether leave off other studies, I yet pursued them with less ardor.

I was quite surprised to find that before a year had elapsed, all who had any desire after purer doctrine were continually coming to me to learn, although I myself was as yet but a mere novice and tyro. Being of a disposition somewhat unpolished and bashful, which led me always to love the shade and retirement, I then began to seek some secluded corner where I might be withdrawn from the public view; but so far from being able to accomplish the object of my desire, all my retreats were like public schools. In short, whilst my one great object was to live in seclusion without being known, God so led me about through different turnings and changes that He never permitted me to rest in any place, until, in spite of my natural disposition, He brought me forth to public notice. Leaving my native country, France, I in fact retired to Germany expressly for the purpose of being able there to enjoy in some obscure corner the repose which I had always desired, and which had been so long denied me. But lo! whilst I lay hidden at Basle and known only to a few people, many faithful and holy persons were burnt alive in France; and the report of these burnings having reached foreign nations, they excited the strongest disapprobation among a great part of the Germans, whose indignation was kindled against the authors of such tyranny. In order to allay this indignation, certain wicked and lying pamphlets were circulated, stating that none were treated with such cruelty but Anabaptists and seditious persons, who by their perverse ravings and false opinions were overthrowing not only religion but also civil order. Observing that the object which these instruments of the court aimed at by their disguises was not only that the disgrace of shedding so much innocent blood might remain buried under false charges and calumnies which they brought against the holy martyrs after their death, but also that afterwards they might be able to proceed to the utmost extremity in murdering the poor saints without exciting compassion towards them in the breasts of any, it appeared to me that unless I opposed them to the utmost of my ability, my silence could not be vindicated from the charge of cowardice and treachery. This was the consideration which induced me to publish my *Institute of the Christian Religion*. My objects were, first, to prove that these reports were false and calumnious, and thus to vindicate my brethren, whose death was precious in the sight of the Lord; and next, that as the same cruelties might very soon after be exercised against many unhappy individuals, foreign nations might be touched with at least some compassion towards them and solicitude about them. When it was then published, it was not that copious and labored work which it now is, but only a small treatise containing a summary of the principal truths of the Christian religion; and it was published with no other design than that men might know what was the faith held by those whom I saw basely and wickedly defamed by those flagitious and perfidious flatterers. That my object was not to acquire fame appeared from [the fact] that immediately afterwards I left Basle, and particularly from the fact that nobody there knew that I was the author.

Wherever else I have gone, I have taken care to conceal that I was the author of that performance; and I had resolved to continue in the same privacy and obscurity until at length William Farel detained me at Geneva, not so much by counsel and exhortation as by a dreadful imprecation, which I felt to be as if God had from heaven laid His mighty hand upon me to arrest me. As the most direct road to Strassburg, to which I then intended to retire, was shut up by the wars, I had resolved to pass quickly by Geneva, without staying longer than a single night in that city. A little before this, popery had been driven from it by the exertions of the excellent person whom I have named, and Peter Viret; but matters were not yet brought to a settled state, and the city was divided into unholy and dangerous factions. Then an individual who now basely apostatized and returned to the papists discovered me and made me known to others. Upon this, Farel, who burned with an extraordinary zeal to advance the gospel, immediately strained every nerve to detain me. And after having learned that my heart was set upon devoting myself to private studies, for which I wished to keep myself free from other pursuits, and finding that he gained nothing by entreaties, he proceeded to utter an imprecation that

God would curse my retirement and the tranquillity of the studies which I sought, if I should withdraw and refuse to give assistance when the necessity was so urgent. By this imprecation I was so stricken with terror that I desisted from the journey which I had undertaken; but sensible of my natural bashfulness and timidity, I would not bring myself under obligation to discharge any particular office. After that, four months had scarcely elapsed when, on the one hand, the Anabaptists began to assail us, and on the other, a certain wicked apostate, . . . secretly supported by the influence of some of the magistrates of the city, was thus enabled to give us a great deal of trouble. At the same time, a succession of dissensions fell out in the city which strangely afflicted us. Being, as I acknowledge, naturally of a timid, soft and pusillanimous disposition, I was compelled to encounter these violent tempests as part of my early training; and although I did not sink under them, yet I was not sustained by such greatness of mind as not to rejoice more than it became me when, in consequence of certain commotions, I was banished from Geneva.

By this means set at liberty and loosed from the tie of my vocation, I resolved to live in a private station, free from the burden and cares of any public charge, when that most excellent servant of Christ, Martin Bucer [reformer in Strassburg], employing a similar kind of remonstrance and protestation as that to which Farel had recourse before, drew me back to a new station. Alarmed by the example of Jonas which he set before me, I still continued in the work of teaching. And although I always continued like myself, studiously avoiding celebrity, yet I was carried, I know not how, as it were by force to the Imperial assemblies, where, willing or unwilling, I was under the necessity of appearing before the eyes of many. Afterwards, when the Lord having compassion on this city had allayed the hurtful agitations and broils which prevailed in it, and by His wonderful power had defeated both the wicked counsels and the sanguinary attempts of the disturbers of the Republic, necessity was imposed upon me of returning to my former charge, contrary to my desire and inclination. The welfare of this church, it is true, lay so near my heart that for its sake I would not have hesitated to lay down my life; but my timidity nevertheless suggested to me many reasons for excusing myself from again willingly taking upon my shoulders so heavy a burden. At length, however, a solemn and conscientious regard to my duty prevailed with me to consent to return to the flock from which I had been torn;

but with what grief, tears, great anxiety and distress I did this, the Lord is my best witness; and many godly persons who would have wished to see me delivered from this painful state, had it not been that which I feared and which made me give my consent, prevented them and shut their mouths.

2. Farel and Calvin: The Geneva Confession

Soon after Calvin's arrival in Geneva, William Farel with Calvin's collaboration prepared the *Confession of Faith* as a summary of central Christian doctrine. It was written in 1536, the same year in which the first edition of Calvin's *Institutes* was published, and it followed the same plan as Calvin's major work. The basic Reformation principle that the source of all Christian teaching must be the Word of God is emphasized in the very first paragraph, where the *sola scriptura* principle is insisted upon. The *Confession* serves as a neat summary of Calvin's doctrinal views. From *Calvin: Theological Treatises* (Volume XXII: The Library of Christian Classics), translated by J.K.S. Reid. Published simultaneously in Great Britain and the U.S.A. by S.C.M. Press Ltd. and The Westminster Press in MCMLIV. Used by permission of Westminster/John Knox Press.

CONFESSION OF FAITH

which all the citizens and inhabitants of Geneva
and the subjects of the country must promise to
keep and hold
(1536)

1. THE WORD OF GOD

First we affirm that we desire to follow Scripture alone as rule of faith and religion, without mixing it with any other thing which might be devised by the opinion of men apart from the Word of

God, and without wishing to accept for our spiritual government any other doctrine than what is conveyed to us by the same Word without addition or diminution, according to the command of our Lord.

2. ONE ONLY GOD

Following, then, the lines laid down in the Holy Scriptures, we acknowledge that there is one only God, Whom we are both to worship and serve, and in *Whom* we are to put all our confidence and hope; having this assurance, that in Him alone is contained all wisdom, power, justice, goodness and pity. And since He is spirit, He is to be served in spirit and in truth. Therefore we think it an abomination to put our confidence or hope in any created thing; to worship anything else than Him, whether angels or any other creatures; and to recognize any other Saviour of our souls than Him alone, whether saints or men living upon earth; and likewise to offer the service which ought to be rendered to Him in external ceremonies or carnal observances, as if He took pleasure in such things; or to make an image to represent His divinity or any other image for adoration.

3. THE LAW OF GOD ALIKE FOR ALL

Because there is one only Lord and Master who has dominion over our consciences, and because His will is the only principle of all justice, we confess all our life ought to be ruled in accordance with the commandments of His holy law in which is contained all perfection of justice, and that we ought to have no other rule of good and just living, nor invent other good works to supplement it than those which are there contained, as follows: Exodus 20: "I am the Lord thy God, who brought thee," and so on.

4. NATURAL MAN

We acknowledge man by nature to be blind, darkened in understanding, and full of corruption and perversity of heart, so that of himself he has no power to be able to comprehend the true knowledge of God as is proper, [nor] to apply himself to good works. But on the contrary, if he is left by God to what he is by nature, he is only able to live in ignorance and to be abandoned to all iniquity. Hence he has need to be illumined by God, so that he come to the right knowledge of his salvation, and thus . . . be re-directed in his affections and reformed to the obedience of the righteousness of God.

5. MAN BY HIMSELF LOST

Since man is naturally (as has been said) deprived and destitute in himself of all the light of God and of all righteousness, we acknowledge that by himself he can only expect the wrath and malediction of God, and hence that he must look outside himself for the means of his salvation.

6. SALVATION IN JESUS

We confess that it is Jesus Christ who is given to us by the Father, in order that in Him we should recover all of which in ourselves we are deficient. Now all that Jesus Christ has done and suffered for our redemption we veritably hold without any doubt, as it is contained in the Creed which is recited in the Church, that is to say: "I believe in God the Father Almighty," and so on.

7. RIGHTEOUSNESS IN JESUS

Therefore we acknowledge the things which are consequently given to us by God in Jesus Christ: first, that being in our own nature enemies of God and subjects of His wrath and judgment, we are reconciled with Him and received again in grace through the intercession of Jesus Christ, so that by His righteousness and guilt-lessness we have remission of our sins, and by the shedding of His blood we are cleansed from all our stains.

8. REGENERATION IN JESUS

Second, we acknowledge that by His Spirit we are regenerated into a new spiritual nature. That is to say that the evil desires of our flesh are mortified by grace, so that they rule us no longer. On the contrary, our will is rendered conformable to God's will, to follow in His way and to seek what is pleasing to Him. Therefore we are by Him delivered from the servitude of sin, under whose power we were of ourselves held captive, and by this deliverance we are made capable and able to do good works and not otherwise.

9. REMISSION OF SINS ALWAYS NECESSARY FOR THE FAITHFUL

Finally, we acknowledge that this regeneration is so effected in us that, until we slough off this mortal body, there remains always in us much imperfection and infirmity, so that we always remain poor and wretched sinners in the presence of God. And, however much we ought day by day to increase and grow in God's righteousness, there will never be plentitude or perfection while we live here. Thus we always have need of the mercy of God to obtain the remission of our faults and offences. And so we ought always to look for our righteousness in Jesus Christ and not at all in ourselves, and in Him be confident and assured, putting no faith in our works.

10. ALL OUR GOOD IN THE GRACE OF GOD

In order that all glory and praise be rendered to God (as is His due), and that we be able to have true peace and rest of conscience, we understand and confess that we receive all benefits from God, as said above, by His clemency and pity, without any consideration of our worthiness or the merit of our works, to which is due no other retribution than eternal confusion. None the less our Saviour in His goodness, having received us into the communion of His son Jesus, regards the works that we have done in faith as pleasing and agreeable; not that they merit it at all, but because, not imputing any of the imperfection that is there, He acknowledges in them nothing but what proceeds from His Spirit.

11. FAITH

We confess that the entrance which we have to the great treasures and riches of the goodness of God that is vouchsafed to us is by faith; inasmuch as, in certain confidence and assurance of heart, we believe in the promises of the gospel, and receive Jesus Christ as He is offered to us by the Father and described to us by the Word of God.

12. INVOCATION OF GOD ONLY AND INTERCESSION OF CHRIST

As we have declared that we have confidence and hope for salvation and all good only in God through Jesus Christ, so we confess that we ought to invoke Him in all necessities in the name of Jesus Christ, who is our mediator and advocate with Him and has access to Him. Likewise we ought to acknowledge that all good things come from Him alone, and to give thanks to Him for them. On the other hand, we reject the intercession of the saints as a superstition invented by men contrary to Scripture, for the reason that it proceeds from mistrust of the sufficiency of the intercession of Jesus Christ.

13. PRAYER INTELLIGIBLE

Moreover since prayer is nothing but hypocrisy and fantasy unless it proceed from the interior affections of the heart, we believe that all prayers ought to be made with clear understanding. And for this reason, we hold the prayer of our Lord to show fittingly what we ought to ask of Him: "Our Father which art in heaven, . . . but deliver us from evil. Amen."

14. SACRAMENTS

We believe that the sacraments which our Lord has ordained in His Church are to be regarded as exercises of faith for us, both for fortifying and confirming it in the promises of God and for witnessing before men. Of them there are in the Christian Church only two which are instituted by the authority of our Saviour; baptism and the supper of our Lord; for what is held within the realm of the pope concerning seven sacraments, we condemn as fable and lie.

15. BAPTISM

Baptism is an external sign by which our Lord testifies that He desires to receive us for His children, as members of His Son Jesus.

Hence in it there is represented to us the cleansing from sin which we have in the blood of Jesus Christ, the mortification of our flesh which we have by His death that we may live in Him by His Spirit. Now since our children belong to such an alliance with our Lord, we are certain that the external sign is rightly applied to them.

16. THE HOLY SUPPER

The supper of our Lord is a sign by which under bread and wine He represents the true spiritual communion which we have in His body and blood. And we acknowledge that according to His ordinance it ought to be distributed in the company of the faithful, in order that all those who wish to have Jesus for their life be partakers of it. Inasmuch as the mass of the pope was a reprobate and diabolical ordinance subverting the mystery of the holy supper, we declare that it is execrable to us, an idolatry condemned by God; for so much is it itself regarded as a sacrifice for the redemption of souls that the bread is in it taken and adored as God. Besides there are other execrable blasphemies and superstitions implied here, and the abuse of the Word of God which is taken in vain without profit or edification.

17. HUMAN TRADITIONS

The ordinances that are necessary for the internal discipline of the Church, and [that] belong solely to the maintenance of peace, honesty and good order in the assembly of Christians, we do not hold to be human traditions at all, inasmuch as they are comprised under the general command of Paul, where he desires that all be done among them decently and in order. But all laws and regulations made binding on conscience which obliged the faithful to things not commanded by God, or [which] establish another service of God than which he demands, thus tending to destroy Christian liberty, we condemn as perverse doctrines of Satan, in view of our Lord's declaration that He is honored in vain by doctrines that are the commandment of men. It is in this estimation that we hold pilgrimages, monasteries, distinctions of foods, prohibition of marriage, confessions and other like things.

18. THE CHURCH

While there is one only Church of Jesus Christ, we always acknowledge that necessity requires companies of the faithful to be
distributed in different places. Of these assemblies each one is called
Church. But inasmuch as all companies do not assemble in the
name of our Lord, but rather to blaspheme and pollute Him by
their sacrilegious deeds, we believe that the proper mark by which
rightly to discern the Church of Jesus Christ is that His holy gospel
be purely and faithfully preached, proclaimed, heard and kept;
that his sacraments be properly administered, even if there be some
imperfections and faults as there always will be among men. On
the other hand, where the gospel is not declared, heard and received, there we do not acknowledge the form of the Church. Hence
the churches governed by the ordinances of the pope are rather
synagogues of the devil than Christian churches.

19. EXCOMMUNICATION

Because there are always some who hold God and His Word in
contempt, who take account of neither injunction, exhortation nor
remonstrance, thus requiring greater chastisement, we hold the
discipline of excommunication to be a thing holy and salutary
among the faithful, since truly it was instituted by our Lord with
good reason. This is in order that the wicked should not by their
damnable conduct corrupt the good and dishonor our Lord, and
that though proud they may turn to penitence. Therefore we believe that it is expedient according to the ordinance of God that all
manifest idolaters, blasphemers, murderers, thieves, lewd persons,
false witnesses, seditionmongers, quarrelers, those guilty of defama-
tion or assault, drunkards, dissolute livers—when they have been
duly admonished and if they do not make amendment, be separated from the communion of the faithful until their repentance
is known.

20. MINISTERS OF THE WORD

We recognize no other pastors in the church than faithful
pastors of the Word of God, feeding the sheep of Jesus Christ on
the one hand with instruction, admonition, consolation, exhortation, deprecation; and on the other resisting all false doctrines

and deceptions of the devil, without mixing with the pure doctrine of the Scriptures their dreams or their foolish imaginings. To these we accord no other power or authority but to conduct, rule and govern the people of God committed to them by the same Word, in which they have power to command, defend, promise and warn, and without which they neither can nor ought to attempt anything. As we receive the true ministers of the Word of God as messengers and ambassadors of God, it is necessary to listen to them as to Him Himself, and we hold their ministry to be a commission from God necessary in the church. On the other hand we hold that all seductive and false prophets, who abandon the purity of the gospel and deviate to their own inventions, ought not at all to be suffered or maintained; who are not the pastors they pretend, but rather, like ravening wolves, ought to be hunted and ejected from the people of God.

21. MAGISTRATES

We hold the supremacy and dominion of kings and princes as also of other magistrates and officers to be a holy thing and a good ordinance of God. And since in performing their office they serve God and follow a Christian vocation, whether in defending the afflicted and innocent, or in correcting and punishing the malice of the perverse, we on our part also ought to accord them honor and reverence, to render respect and subservience, to execute their commands, to bear the charges they impose on us so far as we are able without offence to God. In sum, we ought to regard them as vicars and lieutenants of God, whom one cannot resist without resisting God himself; and their office as a sacred commission from God which has been given them so that they may rule and govern us. Hence we hold that all Christians are bound to pray God for the prosperity of the superiors and lords of the country where they live, to obey the statutes and ordinances which do not contravene the commandments of God, to promote welfare, peace and public good, endeavoring to sustain the honor of those over them and the peace of the people, without contriving or attempting anything to inspire trouble or dissension. On the other hand we declare that all those who conduct themselves unfaithfully towards their superiors, and have not a right concern for the public good of the country where they live, demonstrate thereby their infidelity towards God.

3. Calvin: Ecclesiastical Ordinances, 1541

As a theologian Calvin's great contribution to the evangelical movement was his systematic statement of Christian dogma in the *Institutes*. As a churchman Calvin's major contribution to Protestantism was the development of a form of Church government which eliminated the episcopal hierarchy and could operate independently from and even in opposition to established state churches. Calvin's effort to organize a form of church government based upon the New Testament resulted in a constitution for the Church of Geneva which set a pattern of presbyterianism, *The Ecclesiastical Ordinances*. When Calvin returned to Geneva from his Strassburg exile on June 13, 1541, at the age of thirty-two, he asked the city councils for a committee to help him draft a constitution for the church. The Little Council appointed six members to help and the work was finished in three weeks. It was approved by the Little Council, the Council of Two Hundred, and finally by the General Assembly on November 20, 1541. From *Calvin: Theological Treatises* (Volume XXII: The Library of Christian Classics), translated by J.K.S. Reid. Published simultaneously in Great Britain and the U.S.A. by S.C.M. Press Ltd. and The Westminster Press in MCMLIV. Used by permission of Westminster/John Knox Press.

There are four orders of office instituted by our Lord for the government of His Church.

First, pastors; then doctors; next elders; and fourth deacons.

Hence if we will have a Church well ordered and maintained we ought to observe this form of government.

As to the pastors, whom Scripture also sometimes calls elders and ministers, their office is to proclaim the Word of God, to instruct, admonish, exhort and censure, both in public and private, to administer the sacraments and to enjoin brotherly corrections along with the elders and colleagues.

Now in order that nothing happen confusedly in the Church, no one is to enter upon this office without a calling. In this it is necessary to consider three things, namely: the principal thing is the examination; then what belongs to the institution of the ministers; third, what ceremony or method of procedure it is good to observe in introducing them to office.

The examination contains two parts, of which the first concerns doctrine—to ascertain whether the candidate for ordination has a good and holy knowledge of Scripture, and also whether he be a fit and proper person to communicate it edifyingly to the people.

Further, to avoid all danger of the candidate holding some false opinion, it will be good that he profess his acceptance and maintenance of the doctrine approved by the Church.

To know whether he is fit to instruct, it would be necessary to proceed by interrogation and by hearing him discuss in private the doctrine of the Lord.

The second part concerns life, to ascertain whether he is of good habits and conducts himself always without reproach. The [necessary] rule of procedure in this matter . . . is very well indicated by Paul.

There follows [the question of whose responsibility it is] . . . to institute pastors.

It will be good in this connection to follow the order of the ancient Church, for it is the only practice which is shown us in Scripture. The order is that ministers first elect such as ought to hold office; afterwards that he be presented to the Council; and if he is found worthy the Council receive and accept him, giving him certification to produce finally to the people when he preaches, in order that he be received by the common consent of the company of the faithful. If he be found unworthy, and show this after due probation, it is necessary to proceed to a new election for the choosing of another.

As to the manner of introducing him, it is good to use the [laying on] of hands, which ceremony was observed by the apostles and then in the ancient Church, providing that it take place without superstition and without offence. But because there has been much superstition in the past and scandal might result, it is better to abstain from it because of the infirmity of the times.

When he is elected, he has to swear in front of the Seigneury. Of this oath there will be a prescribed form, suitable to what is required of a minister.

Now as it is necessary to examine the ministers well when they are to be elected, so also it is necessary to have good supervision to maintain them in their duty.

First it will be expedient that all the ministers, for [the purpose of] conserving purity and concord of doctrine among themselves, meet together one certain day each week [to] discuss . . . the Scriptures; and none are to be exempt from this without legitimate excuse. If anyone be negligent, let him be admonished.

As for those who preach in the villages throughout the Seigneury, they are to be exhorted to come as often as they are able. For the rest, if they default an entire month, it is to be held to be very great negligence, unless it is a case of illness or other legitimate hindrance.

If there appear difference of doctrine, let the ministers come together to discuss the matter. Afterwards, if need be, let them call the elders to assist in composing the contention. Finally, if they are unable to come to friendly agreement because of the obstinacy of one of the parties, let the case be referred to the magistrate to be put in order.

To obviate all scandals of living, it will be proper that there be a form of correction to which all submit themselves. It will also be the means by which the ministry may retain respect, and the Word of God be neither dishonored nor scorned because of the ill reputation of the ministers. For as one is to correct those who merit it, so it will be proper to reprove calumnies and false reports which are made unjustly against innocent people.

But first it should be noted that there are crimes which are quite intolerable in a minister, and there are faults which may on the other hand be endured while direct fraternal admonitions are offered.

Of the first sort are:

Heresy, schism, rebellion against ecclesiastical order, blasphemy open and meriting civil punishment, simony and all corruption in presentations, intrigue to occupy another's place, leaving one's Church without lawful leave or just calling, duplicity, perjury, lewdness, larceny, drunkenness, assault meriting punishment by law, usury, games forbidden by the law and scandalous, dances and similar dissoluteness, crimes carrying with them loss of civil rights, crime giving rise to another separation from the Church.

Of the second sort are:

Strange methods of treating Scripture which turn to scandal, curiosity in investigating idle questions, advancing some doctrine or kind of practice not received in the Church, negligence in studying and reading the Scriptures, negligence in rebuking vice amounting to flattery, negligence in doing everything required by his office, scurrility, lying, slander, dissolute words, injurious words, foolhardiness and evil devices, avarice and too great parsimony, undisciplined anger, quarrels and contentions, laxity either of manner or of gesture and like conduct improper to a minister.

In the case of the crimes which cannot at all be tolerated, if some accusation and complaint arise, let the assembly of ministers and elders investigate it, in order to proceed reasonably and according to whatever is discovered in judging the case; and then report judgment to the magistrate in order that if required the delinquent be deposed.

In the case of the lesser vices which may be corrected by simple admonition, one is to proceed according to the command of our Lord, so that as a last step it come for ecclesiastical judgment.

To keep this discipline in operation, let the ministers every three months take special notice whether there be anything to discuss among themselves, to remedy it as is reasonable.

[Concerning] of the number, place and time of preachings

Each Sunday there is to be sermon at St. Peter and St. Gervais at break of day, and at the usual hour at the said St. Peter and St. Gervais.

At midday there is to be catechism, that is, instruction of little children in all the three churches, the Magdalene, St. Peter and St. Gervais.

At three o'clock second sermon in St. Peter and St. Gervais.

For bringing children to catechism and for receiving the sacraments the boundaries of the parishes should as far as possible be observed; that is, St. Gervais embracing what it had in the past;

the Magdalene similarly; St. Peter what belonged formerly to St. Germain, St. Cross, Our Lady the New and St. Legier.

Besides the two preachings which take place, on working days there will be a sermon at St. Peter three times a week, on Monday, Tuesday and Friday, one hour before beginning is made at the other places.

To maintain these charges and others pertaining to the ministry, it will be necessary to have five ministers and three coadjutors who will also be ministers, to aid and assist as necessity requires.

Concerning the second order which we have called Doctors

The office proper to doctors is the instruction of the faithful in true doctrine, in order that the purity of the gospel be not corrupted either by ignorance or by evil opinions. As things are disposed today, we always include under this title aids and instructions for maintaining the doctrine of God and defending the Church from injury by fault of pastors and ministers. So to use a more intelligible word, we will call this the order of the schools.

The degree nearest to the minister and most closely joined to the government of the Church is the lecturer in theology, of which it will be good to have one in Old Testament and one in New Testament.

But because it is only possible to profit from such lectures if first one is instructed in the languages and humanities; and also because it is necessary to raise offspring for time to come, in order not to leave the Church deserted to our children; a college should be instituted for instructing children to prepare them for the ministry as well as for civil government.

For the first, a proper place ought to be assigned both for doing lessons and [for] accommodating the children and others who would profit. There must be a man learned and expert in arranging both the house and the instruction, who is able also to lecture. He is to be chosen and remunerated on condition that he have under his charge lecturers both in languages and in dialectic, if it can be done. Likewise there should be some matriculated persons to teach the little children; and these we hope shortly to appoint to assist the master.

All who are there will be subject like ministers to ecclesiastical discipline.

There need be no other school in the city for the little children, but let the girls have their school apart, as has hitherto been the case.

Let no one be received if he is not approved by the ministers on their testimony, for fear of impropriety.

Concerning the third order which is that of Elders

Their office is to have oversight of the life of everyone, to admonish amicably those whom they see to be erring or to be living a disordered life, and, where it is required, to enjoin fraternal corrections themselves and along with others.

In the present condition of the Church it would be good to elect two of the Little Council, four of the Council of Sixty, and six of the Council of Two Hundred; men of good and honest life, without reproach and beyond suspicion, and above all fearing God and possessing spiritual prudence. These should be so elected that there be some in every quarter of the city, to keep an eye on everybody.

The best way of electing them seems to be this: that the Little Council suggest the nomination of the best that can be found and the most suitable; and to do this, summon the ministers to confer with them; after this they should present those whom they would commend to the Council of Two Hundred, which will approve them. If it find them worthy, let them take the special oath, whose form will be readily drawn up. And at the end of the year, let them present themselves to the Seigneury for consideration whether they ought to be continued or changed. It is inexpedient that they be changed often without cause, so long as they discharge their duty faithfully.

[Concerning] the fourth order of ecclesiastical government, that is, the Deacons

There were always two kinds [of deacons] in the ancient Church, the one deputed to receive, dispense and hold goods for the poor, not only daily alms but also possessions, rents and pensions; the other to tend and care for the sick and administer allowances to the poor. This custom we follow again now for we have procurators and hospitalers.

The number of procurators appointed for this hospital seems to us to be proper; but we wish that there be also a separate reception office, not only so that provisions be in time made better, but [also so] that those who wish to do some charity may be more certain that the gift will not be employed otherwise than they intend. And if the revenue assigned by their Lordships be insufficient, or should extraordinary necessity arise, the Seigneury will advise about adjustment, according to the need they see.

The election of both procurators and hospitalers is to take place like that of the elders; and in electing them the rule proposed by Paul for deacons is to be followed.

With regard to the office of procurator, we think the rules which have already been imposed on them by us are good; by means of which, in urgent affairs, and where there is danger in deferment, and chiefly when there is no grave difficulty or question of great expense, they are not obliged always to be meeting, but one or two can do what is reasonable in the absence of others.

It will be their duty to watch diligently that the public hospital is well maintained, and that this be so both for the sick and the old people unable to work, widowed women, orphaned children and other poor creatures. The sick are always to be lodged in a set of rooms separate from the other people who are unable to work: old men, widowed women, orphaned children and the other poor.

Moreover, care for the poor dispersed through the city should be revived, as the procurators may arrange it.

Moreover, besides the hospital for those passing through which must be maintained, there should be some attention given to any recognized as worthy of special charity. For this purpose, a special room should be set aside to receive those who ought to be assisted by the procurators, which is to be reserved for this business. It should above all be demanded that the families of the hospitalers be honorably ruled in accordance with the will of God since they have to govern houses dedicated to God.

The ministers must on their side inquire whether there be any lack or want of anything, in order to ask and desire the Seigneury to put it in order. To do this, some of their company with the procurators should visit the hospital every three months to ascertain if all is in order.

It would be good, not only for the poor of the hospital but also for those of the city who cannot help themselves, that they have a doctor and a surgeon of their own who should still practice in the city, but meanwhile be required to have care of the hospital and to visit the other poor.

As for the hospital for plague, it should be wholly separate and apart, and especially if it happens that the city be visited by this scourge of God.

For the rest, to discourage mendicancy which is contrary to good order, it would be well, and we have so ordered it, that there be one of our officials at the entrance of the churches to remove from the place those who loiter; and if there be any who give offense or offer insolence to bring them to one of the Lords Syndic. Similarly for the rest of the time, let the Overseers of Tens take care that the total prohibition of begging be well observed.

4. Calvin: The Institutes

Calvin was one of the most prolific authors in the history of the Church, comparable in productivity to Augustine, Aquinas, and Luther. To know Calvin well requires extensive reading in his sermons, treatises, letters, and especially his Biblical commentaries. And yet in a special sense Calvin was a man of one book; his remarkable *Institutes of the Christian Religion* is a systematic presentation of Christian theology which he constantly improved and enlarged from the first edition in 1536 to the last edition which left his hand in the late summer of 1559. He was a young man of twenty-six when he dedicated the first edition to King Francis I of France with a plea for understanding and defense against the persecutors of the French evangelicals. The second edition of 1539 was twice the size of the first; and the final edition, from which the following excerpts are translated, was twice the size of its immediate predecessor. This huge eighth edition was based upon a masterful knowledge of the Scriptures and the Church fathers. The three subjects represented here have not been selected because they are central to the theological heart of the work: for that the student must read on the knowledge of God, in the person and work of Christ, on justification, and on the church. They are chosen rather because of contemporary historical interest in the impact of Calvin's teaching on predestination, vocation, and civil government upon western culture. From *Calvin: Institutes of the Christian Religion* (Volume XX and XXI: The Library of Christian Classics), edited by John T. McNeill and translated by Ford Lewis Battles. Copyright © MCMLX W.L. Jenkins. Used by permission of Westminster/John Knox Press._

Necessity and beneficial effect of the Doctrine of Election; danger of curiosity

In actual fact, the covenant of life is not preached equally among all men, and among those to whom it is preached it does not gain the same acceptance either constantly or in equal degree. In this diversity the wonderful depth of God's judgment is made known. For there is no doubt that this variety also serves the decision of God's eternal election. If it is plain that it comes to pass by God's bidding that salvation is freely offered to some while others are barred from access to it, at once great and difficult questions spring up, explicable only when reverent minds regard as settled what they may suitably hold concerning election and predestination. A baffling question this seems to many. For they think nothing more inconsistent than that out of the common multitude of men some should be predestined to salvation, others to destruction. But how mistakenly they entangle themselves will become clear in the following discussion. Besides, in the very darkness that frightens them not only is the usefulness of this doctrine made known but also its very sweet fruit. We shall never be clearly persuaded, as we ought to be, that our salvation flows from the wellspring of God's free mercy until we come to know His eternal election, which illumines God's grace by this contrast: that He does not indiscriminately adopt all into the hope of salvation but gives to some what He denies to others.

How much the ignorance of this principle detracts from God's glory, how much it takes away from true humility, is well known. Yet Paul denies that this which needs so much to be known can be known unless God, utterly disregarding works, chooses those whom He has decreed within Himself. "At the present time," he says, "a remnant has been saved according to the election of grace. But if it is by grace, it is no more of works; otherwise grace would no more be grace. But if it is of works, it is no more of grace; otherwise work would not be work" [Rom. 11:5-6]. If—to make it clear that our salvation comes about solely from God's mere generosity—we must be called back to the course of election, those who wish to get rid of all this are obscuring as maliciously as they can what ought to have been gloriously and vociferously proclaimed, and they tear humility up by the very roots. Paul clearly testifies that when the salvation of a remnant of the people is ascribed to the election of grace, then only is it acknowledged that God of His mere good pleasure preserves whom He will, and moreover that He pays no reward, since He can owe none.

They who shut the gates that no one may dare seek a taste of this doctrine wrong men no less than God. For neither will anything else suffice to make us humble as we ought to be nor shall we otherwise sincerely feel how much we are obliged to God. And as Christ teaches, here is our only ground for firmness and confidence: in order to free us of all fear and render us victorious amid so many dangers, snares and mortal struggles, He promises that whatever the Father has entrusted into His keeping will be safe [John 10:28-29]. From this we infer that all those who do not know that they are God's own will be miserable through constant fear. Hence those, who by being blind to the three benefits we have noted would wish the foundation of our salvation to be removed from our midst, very badly serve the interests of themselves and of all other believers. How is it that the Church becomes manifest to us from this, when, as Bernard rightly teaches, "it could not otherwise be found or recognized among creatures, since it lies marvelously hidden . . . both within the bosom of a blessed predestination and within the mass of miserable condemnation"?

But before I enter into the matter itself, I need to mention by way of preface two kinds of men.

Human curiosity renders the discussion of predestination, already somewhat difficult of itself, very confusing and even dangerous. No restraints can hold it back from wandering in forbidden bypaths and thrusting upward to the heights. If allowed, it will leave no secret to God that it will not search out and unravel. Since we see so many on all sides rushing into this audacity and impudence, among them certain men not otherwise bad, they should in due season be reminded of the measure of their duty in this regard.

First, then, let them remember that when they inquire into predestination they are penetrating the sacred precincts of divine wisdom. If anyone with carefree assurance breaks into this place, he will not succeed in satisfying his curiosity and he will enter a labyrinth from which he can find no exit. For it is not right for man unrestrainedly to search out things that the Lord has willed to be hid in Himself, and to unfold from eternity itself the sublimest wisdom, which He would have us revere but not understand that through this also He should fill us with wonder. He has set forth by His Word the secrets of His will that He has decided to reveal to us. These He decided to reveal insofar as He foresaw that they would concern us and benefit us.

Doctrine of Predestination to be sought in Scripture only

"We have entered the pathway of faith," says Augustine. "Let us hold steadfastly to it. It leads us to the King's chamber, in which are hid all the treasures of knowledge and wisdom. For the Lord Christ Himself did not bear a grudge against His great and most select disciples when He said: 'I have . . . many things to say to you, but you cannot bear them now' [John 16:12]. We must walk, we must advance, we must grow, that our hearts may be capable of those things which we cannot yet grasp. But if the Last Day finds us advancing, there we shall learn what we could not learn here." If this thought prevails with us, that the Word of the Lord is the sole way that can lead us in our search for all that it is lawful to hold concerning Him, and is the sole light to illumine our vision of all that we should see of Him, it will readily keep and restrain us from all rashness. For we shall know [that] the moment we exceed the bounds of the Word our course is outside the pathway and in darkness, and that there we must repeatedly wander, slip and stumble. Let this, therefore, [be] first of all before our eyes: to seek any other knowledge of predestination than what the Word of God discloses is not less insane than if one should purpose to walk in a pathless waste [cf. Job 12:24], or to see in darkness. And let us not be ashamed to be ignorant of something in this matter, wherein there is a certain learned ignorance. Rather, let us willingly refrain from inquiring into a kind of knowledge, the ardent desire for which is both foolish and dangerous, nay, even deadly. But if a wanton curiosity agitates us, we shall always do well to oppose to it this restraining thought: just as too much honey is not good, so for the curious the investigation of glory is not turned into glory [Prov. 25:27]. For there is good reason for us to be deterred from this insolence which can only plunge us into ruin. . . .

Summary survey of the Doctrine of Election

As Scripture, then, clearly shows, we say that God once established by His eternal and unchangeable plan those whom He long before determined once for all to receive into salvation, and those whom, on the other hand, he would devote to destruction. We assert that, with respect to the elect, this plan was founded upon His freely given mercy, without regard to human worth; but by His just and irreprehensible but incomprehensible judgment He has barred the door of life to those whom He has given over to damnation. Now among the elect we regard the call as a

testimony of election. Then we hold justification another sign of
its manifestation, until they come into the glory in which the ful-
fillment of that election lies. But as the Lord seals His elect by
call and justification, so, by shutting off the reprobate from knowledge of His name or from the sanctification of His Spirit, he, as
it were, reveals by these marks what sort of judgment awaits them.
Here I shall pass over many fictions that stupid men have invented
to overthrow predestination. They need no refutation, for as soon
as they are brought forth they abundantly prove their own falsity.
I shall pause only over those which either are being argued by
the learned or may raise difficulty for the simple, or which impiety
speciously sets forth in order to assail God's righteousness.

How we must use the Present Life and its helps

1. DOUBLE DANGER: MISTAKEN STRICTNESS
AND MISTAKEN LAXITY

By such elementary instruction, Scripture at the same time
duly informs us what is the right use of earthly benefits—a
matter not to be neglected in the ordering of our life. For if we
are to live, we have also to use those helps necessary for living.
And we also cannot avoid those things which seem to serve delight more than necessity. Therefore we must hold to a measure
so as to use them with a clear conscience, whether for necessity
or for delight. By His word the Lord lays down this measure when
He teaches that the present life is for his people as a pilgrimage
on which they are hastening toward the heavenly kingdom [Lev.
25:23; I Chron. 29:15; Ps. 39:13; 119:19; Heb. 11:8-10, 13-16;
13:14; I Peter 2:11]. If we must simply pass through this world,
there is no doubt we ought to use its good things insofar as they
help rather than hinder our course. Thus Paul rightly persuades
us to use this world as if not using it; and to buy goods with the
same attitude as one sells them [I Cor. 7:30-31].

But because this topic is a slippery one and slopes on both sides
into error, let us try to plant our feet where we may safely stand.
There were some otherwise good and holy men who when they
say intemperance and wantonness, when not severely restrained,

ever raging with unbridled excess, desired to correct this dangerous evil. This one plan occurred to them: they allowed man to
use physical goods insofar as necessity required. A godly counsel
indeed, but they were far too severe. For they would fetter consciences more tightly than does the Word of the Lord—a very
dangerous thing. Now to them necessity means to abstain from
all things that they could do without; thus, according to them,
it would scarcely be permitted to add any food at all to plain
bread and water. And others are even more severe. We are told
of Crates the Theban that he cast all his goods into the sea; for
he thought that unless they were destroyed, they would destroy
him.

But many today, while they seek an excuse for the intemperance
of the flesh in its use of external things, and while they would
meanwhile pave the road to licentious indulgence, take for granted
what I do not at all concede to them: that this freedom is not to
be restrained by any limitation but to be left to every man's conscience to use as far as seems lawful to him. Certainly I admit that
consciences neither ought to nor can be bound here to definite and
precise legal formulas; but inasmuch as Scripture gives general
rules for lawful use, we ought surely to limit our use in accordance
with them.

2. THE MAIN PRINCIPLE

Let this be our principle: that the use of God's gifts is not
wrongly directed when it is referred to that end to which the
Author Himself created and destined them for us, since he created
them for our good, not for our ruin. Accordingly, no one will hold
to a straighter path than he who diligently looks to this end. Now
if we ponder to what end God created food, we shall find that He
meant not only to provide for necessity but also for delight and
good cheer. Thus the purpose of clothing, apart from necessity, was
comeliness and decency. In grasses, trees and fruits, apart from
their various uses there is beauty of appearance and pleasantness of
odor [cf. Gen. 2:9]. For if this were not true, the prophet would
not have reckoned them among the benefits of God, "that wine
gladdens the heart of man, that oil makes his face shine" [Ps.
104:15]. Scripture would not have reminded us repeatedly, in com-
mending His kindness, that He gave all such things to men. And

the natural qualities themselves of things demonstrate sufficiently to what end and extent we may enjoy them. Has the Lord clothed the flowers with the great beauty that greets our eyes, the sweetness of smell that is wafted upon our nostrils, and yet will it be unlawful for our eyes to be affected by that beauty, or our sense of smell by the sweetness of that odor? What? Did He not so distinguish colors as to make some more lovely than others? What? Did He not endow gold and silver, ivory and marble, with a loveliness that renders them more precious than other metals or stones? Did He not, in short, render many things attractive to us, apart from their necessary use?

3. A LOOK AT THE GIVER OF THE GIFT PREVENTS NARROW-MINDEDNESS AND IMMODERATION

Away, then, with that inhuman philosophy which, while conceding only a necessary use of creatures, not only malignantly deprives us of the lawful fruit of God's beneficence but cannot be practiced unless it robs a man of all his senses and degrades him to a block.

But no less diligently, on the other hand, we must resist the lust of the flesh, which, unless it is kept in order, overflows without measure. And it has, as I have said, its own advocates, who under the pretext of the freedom conceded permit everything to it. First, one bridle is put upon it if it be determined that all things were created for us that we might recognize the Author and give thanks for His kindness toward us. Where is your thanksgiving if you so gorge yourself with banqueting or wine that you either become stupid or are rendered useless for the duties of piety and of your calling? Where is your recognition of God if your flesh, boiling over with excessive abundance [of] vile lust, infects the mind with its impurity so that you cannot discern anything that is right and honorable? Where is our gratefulness toward God for our clothing if in the sumptuousness of our apparel we both admire ourselves and despise others, if with its elegance and glitter we prepare ourselves for shameless conduct? Where is our recognition of God if our minds be fixed upon the splendor of our apparel? For many so enslave all their senses to delights that the mind lies overwhelmed. Many are so delighted with marble, gold and pictures that they become marble; they turn, as it were, into metals and are like painted figures. The smell of the kitchen or the sweetness of its odors so stupifies others that they are unable to smell anything spiritual. The same thing is also to be seen in other matters. Therefore, clearly, leave to abuse God's gifts must be somewhat curbed, and Paul's rule is confirmed: that we should "make no provision for the flesh, to gratify its desires" [Rom. 13:14], for if we yield too much to these, they boil up without measure or control.

4. ASPIRATION TO ETERNAL LIFE ALSO DETERMINES ARIGHT OUR OUTWARD CONDUCT OF LIFE

But there is no surer or more direct course than that which we receive from contempt of the present life and meditation upon heavenly immortality. For from this two rules follow: those who use this world should be so affected as if they did not use it; those who marry, as if they did not marry; those who buy, as if they did not buy, just as Paul enjoins [1 Cor. 7:29-31]. The other rule is that they should know how to bear poverty peaceably and patiently, as well as to bear abundance moderately. He who bids you use this world as if you used it not destroys not only the intemperance of gluttony in food and drink, and excessive indulgence at table, in buildings and clothing, ambition, pride, arrogance and overfastidiousness, but also all care and inclination that either diverts or hinders you from thought of the heavenly life and zeal to cultivate the soul. Long ago Cato truly said: "There is great care about dress, but great carelessness about virtue." To use the old proverb: those who are much occupied with the care of the body are for the most part careless about their own souls.

Therefore, even though the freedom of believers in external matters is not to be restricted to a fixed formula, yet it is surely subject to this law: to indulge oneself as little as possible; but, on the contrary, with unflagging effort of mind to insist upon cutting off all show of superfluous wealth, not to mention licentiousness, and diligently to guard against turning helps into hindrances.

5. FRUGALITY, EARTHLY POSSESSIONS HELD IN TRUST

The second rule will be: they who have narrow and slender resources should know how to go without things patiently, lest they be troubled by an immoderate desire for them. If they keep this rule of moderation, they will make considerable progress in the Lord's school. So, too, they who have not progressed, in some degree at least, in this respect have scarcely anything to prove them disciples of Christ. For besides the fact that most other vices accompany the desire for earthly things, he who bears poverty impatiently also when in prosperity commonly betrays the contrary disease. This is my point: he who is ashamed of mean clothing will boast of costly clothing; he who, not content with a slender meal is troubled by the desire for a more elegant one, will also intemperately abuse those elegances if they fall to his lot. He who will bear reluctantly and with a troubled mind his deprivation and humble condition, if he be advanced to honors will by no means abstain from arrogance. To this end, then, let all those for whom the pursuit of piety is not a pretense strive to learn, by the apostle's example, how to be filled and to hunger, to abound and to suffer want [Phil. 4:12].

Besides, Scripture has a third rule with which to regulate the use of earthly things. Of it we said something when we discussed the precepts of love. It decrees that all those things were so given to us by the kindness of God and so destined for our benefit that they are, as it were, entrusted to us, and we must one day render account of them. Thus, therefore, we must so arrange it that this saying may continually resound in our ears: "Render account of your stewardship" [Luke 16:2]. At the same time let us remember by whom such reckoning is required: namely, Him Who has greatly commended abstinence, sobriety, frugality and moderation; and has also abominated excess, pride, ostentation and vanity; Who approves no other distribution of good things than one joined with love; Who has already condemned with His own lips all delights that draw man's spirit away from chastity and purity, or befog his mind.

6. THE LORD'S CALLING A BASIS OF OUR WAY OF LIFE

Finally, this point is to be noted: the Lord bids each one of us in all life's actions to look to His calling. For He knows with what great restlessness human nature flames, with what fickleness it is borne hither and thither, how its ambition longs to embrace various things at once. Therefore, lest through our stupidity and rashness everything be turned topsy-turvy, He has appointed duties for every man in his particular way of life. And that no one may thoughtlessly transgress his limits, He has named these various kinds of living "callings." Therefore each individual has his own kind of living assigned to him by the Lord as a sort of sentry post so that he may not heedlessly wander about throughout life. Now so necessary is this distinction that all our actions are judged in His sight by it, often indeed far otherwise than in the judgment of human and philosophical reason. No deed is considered more noble, even among philosophers, than to free one's country from tyranny. Yet a private citizen who lays his hand upon a tyrant is openly condemned by the heavenly judge [1 Sam. 24:7, 11; 26:9].

But I will not delay to list examples. It is enough if we know that the Lord's calling is in everything the beginning and foundation of well-doing. And if there is anyone who will not direct himself to it, he will never hold to the straight path in his duties. Perhaps sometimes he could contrive something laudable in appearance; but whatever it may be in the eyes of men, it will be rejected before God's throne. Besides, there will be no harmony among the several parts of his life. Accordingly, your life will then be best ordered when it is directed to this goal. For no one, impelled by his own rashness, will attempt more than his calling will permit, because he will know that it is not lawful to exceed its bounds. A man of obscure station will lead a private life ungrudgingly so as not to leave the rank in which he has been placed by God. Again, it will be no slight relief from cares, labors, troubles and other burdens for a man to know that God is his guide in all these things. The magistrate will discharge his functions more willingly; the head of the household will confine himself to his duty; each man will bear and swallow the discomforts, vexations, weariness and anxieties in his way of life when he has been persuaded that the burden was laid upon him by God. From this will arise also a singular consolation: that no task will be so sordid and base, provided you obey your calling in it, that it will not shine and be reckoned very precious in God's sight.

Civil Government

1. DIFFERENCES BETWEEN SPIRITUAL
AND CIVIL GOVERNMENT

Now, since we have established above that man is under a two-fold government, and since we have elsewhere discussed at sufficient length the kind that resides in the soul or inner man and pertains to eternal life, this is the place to say something also about the other kind, which pertains only to the establishment of civil justice and outward morality.

For although this topic seems by nature alien to the spiritual doctrine of faith which I have undertaken to discuss, what follows will show that I am right in joining them, in fact that necessity compels me to do so. This is especially true since, from one side, insane and barbarous men furiously strive to overturn this divinely established order; while, on the other side, the flatterers of princes, immoderately praising their power, do not hesitate to set them against the rule of God himself. Unless both these evils are checked, purity of faith will perish. Besides, it is of no slight importance to us to know how lovingly God has provided in this respect for mankind, that greater zeal for piety may flourish in us to attest our gratefulness.

First, before we enter into the matter itself, we must keep in mind that distinction which we previously laid down so that we do not (as commonly happens) unwisely mingle these two, which have a completely different nature. For certain men, when they hear that the gospel promises a freedom that acknowledges no king and no magistrate among men, but looks to Christ alone, think that they cannot benefit by their freedom so long as they see any power set up over them. They therefore think that nothing will be safe unless the whole world is reshaped to a new form, where there are neither courts, nor laws, nor magistrates, nor anything which in their opinion restricts their freedom. But whoever knows how to distinguish between body and soul, between this present fleeting life and that future eternal life, will without difficulty know that Christ's spiritual kingdom and the civil jurisdiction are things completely distinct. Since, then, it is a Jewish vanity to seek and enclose Christ's kingdom within the elements of this world, let us rather ponder that what Scripture clearly teaches is a spiritual fruit which we gather from Christ's grace; and let us remember to keep within its own limits all that freedom which is promised and offered to us in Him. For why is it that the same apostle who bids us stand and not submit to the "yoke of bondage" [Gal. 5:1] elsewhere forbids slaves to be anxious about their state [I Cor. 7:21], unless it be that spiritual freedom can perfectly well exist along with civil bondage? These statements of His must also be taken in the same sense: In the kingdom of God "there is neither Jew nor Greek, neither male nor female, neither slave nor free" [Gal. 3:28; order changed]. And again, "there is not Jew nor Greek, uncircumcised and circumcised, barbarian, Scythian, slave, freeman; but Christ is all in all" [Col. 3:11]. By these statements He means that it makes no difference what your condition among men may be or under what nation's laws you live, since the kingdom of Christ does not at all consist in these things.

2. THE TWO "GOVERNMENTS" ARE NOT ANTITHETICAL

Yet this distinction does not lead us to consider the whole nature of government a thing polluted, which has nothing to do with Christian men. That is what, indeed, certain fanatics who delight in unbridled license shout and boast: after we have died through Christ to the elements of this world [Col. 2:20], are transported to God's kingdom and sit among heavenly beings, it is a thing unworthy of us and set far beneath our excellence to be occupied with those vile and worldly cares which have to do with business foreign to a Christian man. To what purpose, they ask, are there laws without trials and tribunals? But what has a Christian man to do with trials themselves? Indeed, if it is not lawful to kill, why do we have laws and trials? But as we have just now pointed out that this kind of government is distinct from that spiritual and inward kingdom of Christ, so we must know that they are not at variance. For spiritual government, indeed, is already initiating in us upon earth certain beginnings of the heavenly kingdom, and in this mortal and fleeting life affords a certain forecast of an immortal and incorruptible blessedness. Yet civil government has as its appointed end, so long as we live among men, to cherish and protect the outward worship of God, to defend sound doctrine of piety and the position of the church, to adjust our life to the society of men, to form our social behavior to civil righteousness, to reconcile us with one another and to promote general peace and tranquility. All of this I admit to be superfluous if God's kingdom, such as it is now among us, wipes out the present life. But if it is God's will that we go as pilgrims upon the earth while we aspire to the true fatherland, and if the pilgrimage requires such helps, those who take these from man deprive him of his very humanity. Our adversaries claim that there ought to be such great perfection in the church of God that its government should suffice for law. But they stupidly imagine such a perfection as can never be found in a community of men. For since the insolence of evil men is so great, their wickedness so stubborn, that it can scarcely be restrained by extremely severe laws, what do we expect them to do if they see that their depravity can go scot-free—when no power can force them to cease from doing evil?

3. THE CHIEF TASKS AND BURDENS OF CIVIL GOVERNMENT

But there will be a more appropriate place to speak of the practice of civil government. Now we only wish it to be understood that to think of doing away with it is outrageous barbarity. Its function among men is no less than that of bread, water, sun and air; indeed, its place of honor is far more excellent. For it does not merely see to it, as all these serve to do, that men breathe, eat, drink and are kept warm, even though it surely embraces all these activities when it provides for their living together. It does not, I repeat, look to this only, but also prevents idolatry, sacrilege against God's name, blasphemies against His truth and other public offenses against religion from arising and spreading among the people; it prevents the public peace from being disturbed; it provides that each man may keep his property safe and sound; that men may carry on blameless intercourse among themselves; that honesty and modesty may be preserved among men. In short, it provides that a public manifestation of religion may exist among Christians and that humanity be maintained among men.

Let no man be disturbed that I now commit to civil government the duty of rightly establishing religion, which I seem above to have put outside of human decision. For when I approve of a civil administration that aims to prevent the true religion which is contained in God's law from being openly and with public sacrilege violated and defiled with impunity, I do not here, any more than before, allow men to make laws according to their own decision concerning religion and the worship of God.

But my readers, assisted by the very clarity of the arrangement, will better understand what is to be thought of the whole subject of civil government if we discuss its parts separately. These are three: the magistrate, who is the protector and guardian of the laws; the laws according to which he governs; the people, who are governed by the laws and obey the magistrate.

Let us, then, first look at the office of the magistrate, noting whether it is a lawful calling approved of God; the nature of the office; the extent of its power; then, with what laws a Christian government ought to be governed; and finally, how the laws benefit the people, and what obedience is owed to the magistrate. . . .

* * *

31. CONSTITUTIONAL DEFENDERS OF THE PEOPLE'S FREEDOM

But however these deeds of men are judged in themselves, still the Lord accomplished His work through them alike when He broke the bloody sceptors of arrogant kings and when He overturned intolerable governments. Let the princes hear and be afraid.

But we must, in the meantime, be very careful not to despise or violate that authority of magistrates, full of venerable majesty, which God has established by the weightiest decrees, even though it may reside with the most unworthy men who defile it as much as they can with their own wickedness. For, if the correction of unbridled despotism is the Lord's to avenge, let us not at once think that it is entrusted to us, to whom no command has been given except to obey and suffer.

I am speaking all the while of private individuals. For if there are now any magistrates of the people, appointed to restrain the willfulness of kings (as in ancient times the ephors were set against the Spartan kings, or the tribunes of the people against the Roman consuls, or the demarchs against the senate of the Athenians; and perhaps, as things now are, such power as the three estates exercise in every realm when they hold their chief assemblies), I am so far from forbidding them to withstand, in accordance with their duty, the fierce licentiousness of kings, that, if they wink at kings who violently fall upon and assault the lowly common folk, I declare that their dissimulation involves nefarious perfidy, because they dishonestly betray the freedom of the people, of which they know that they have been appointed protectors by God's ordinance.

32. OBEDIENCE TO MAN MUST NOT BECOME DISOBEDIENCE TO GOD

But in that obedience which we have shown to be due the authority of rulers, we are always to make this exception; indeed, to observe it as primary, that such obedience is never to lead us away from obedience to Him to Whose will the desires of all kings ought to be subject, to Whose decrees all their commands ought to yield, to Whose majesty their sceptors ought to be submitted. And how absurd would it be that in satisfying men you should incur the displeasure of Him for whose sake you obey men themselves! The Lord, therefore, is the King of Kings, Who, when He has opened His sacred mouth, must alone be heard, before all and above all men; next to him we are subject to those men who are in authority over us, but only in Him. If they command anything against Him, let it go unesteemed. And here let us not be concerned about all that dignity which the magistrates possess; for no harm is done to it when it is humbled before that singular and truly supreme power of God.

On this consideration, Daniel denies that he has committed any offense against the king when he has not obeyed his impious edict [Dan. 6:22-23]. For the king had exceeded his limits, and had not only been a wrongdoer against men, but, in lifting up his horns against God, had himself abrogated his power. Conversely, the Israelites are condemned because they were too obedient to the wicked proclamation of the king [Hos. 5:13]. For when Jeroboam molded the golden calves, they, to please him, forsook God's temple and turned to new superstitions [I Kings 12:30]. With the same readiness, their descendants complied with the decrees of their kings. The prophet sharply reproaches them for embracing the king's edicts [Hos. 5:11]. Far, indeed, is the pretense of modesty from deserving praise, a false modesty with which the court flatterers cloak themselves and deceive the simple, while they deny that it is lawful for them to refuse anything imposed by their kings. As if God had made over His right to mortal men, giving them the rule over mankind! Or as if earthly power were diminished when it is subjected to its Author, in Whose presence even the heavenly powers tremble as suppliants! I know with what great and present peril this constancy is menaced, because kings bear defiance with the greatest displeasure, whose "wrath is a messenger of death," says Solomon [Prov. 16:14]. But since this edict has been proclaimed by the heavenly herald, Peter—"We must obey God rather than men" [Acts 5:29]—let us comfort ourselves with the thought that we are rendering that obedience which the Lord requires when we suffer anything rather than turn aside from piety. And that our courage may not grow faint, Paul pricks us with another goad: That we have been redeemed by Christ at so great a price as our redemption cost Him, so that we should not enslave ourselves to the wicked desires of men—much less be subject to their impiety [I Cor. 7:23].

God Be Praised

5. Calvin: Letter to the Five Prisoners of Lyons

Calvin's remarkable talent for organization extended far beyond the confines of Geneva and the Swiss cantons. His vast correspondence reveals that he was in close touch with developments in all parts of Europe and maintained personal contact with Reformed ministers and missionaries also in Catholic territories. The letter which follows is a moving testimony to Calvin's concern for five young French martyrs. In April, 1552, five young French Protestants completed a course of theological instruction at Lausanne and after spending a few days in Geneva set out for Lyons, France. They met a stranger on the way who invited them to visit his home, where they were arrested, taken to prison, tried and condemned to death. During their imprisonment Calvin wrote to express the sympathy of the church in Geneva. From *Letters of John Calvin*, II, Jules Bonnet, ed. (Edinburgh: Thomas Constable and Co., 1857), pp. 335-336, 338.

To the Five Prisoners of Lyons,—Martial Alba, Peter Escrivain, Charles Favre, Peter Navihères, Bernard Seguin.

From Geneva, this 10th of June, 1552.

My very dear Brethren,—Hitherto I have put off writing to you, fearing that if the letter fell into bad hands it might give fresh occasion to the enemy to afflict you. And besides, I have been informed how that God wrought so powerfully in you by His grace, that you stood in no great need of my letters. However, we have not forgotten you, neither I nor all the brethren hereabouts, as to whatever we have been able to do for you. As soon as you were taken, we heard of it and knew how it had come to pass. We took care that help might be sent you with all speed, and are now waiting the result. Those who have influence with the prince in whose power God has put your lives are faithfully exerting themselves on your behalf, but we do not yet know how far they have succeeded in their suit. Meanwhile, all the children of God pray for you as they are bound to do, not only on account of the mutual compassion which ought to exist between members of the same body, but because they know well that you labor for them in maintaining the cause of their salvation. We hope, come what may, that God of His goodness will give a happy issue to your captivity, so that we shall have reason to rejoice. You see to what He has called you; doubt not, therefore, that according as He employs you, He will give you strength to fulfill His work, for He has promised this, and we know by experience that He has never failed those who allow themselves to be governed by Him. Even now you have proof of this in yourselves, for He has shown His power by giving you so much constancy in withstanding the first assaults. Be confident, therefore, that He will not leave the work of His hand imperfect. You know what Scripture sets before us, to encourage us to fight for the cause of the Son of God; meditate upon what you have both heard and seen formerly on this head, so as to put it in practice. For all that I could say would be of little service to you, were it not drawn from this fountain. And truly we have need of a much more firm support than that of men, to make us victorious over such strong enemies as the devil, death and the world; but the firmness which is in Christ Jesus is sufficient for this and all else that might shake us were we not established in Him. Knowing, then, in whom ye have believed, manifest what authority He deserves to have over you. . . .

In conclusion, I beseech our good Lord that He would be pleased to make you feel in every way the worth of His protection of His own; to fill you with His Holy Spirit, who gives you prudence and virtue, and brings you peace, joy and contentment; and may the name of our Lord Jesus be glorified by you to the edification of His Church!

Part Five

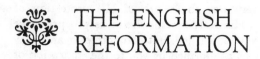

THE ENGLISH REFORMATION

1. Fish: A Supplication of Beggars

The English Reformation is so often thought of in terms of
the King's great question and Acts of Parliament that the
popular furor and rage of the masses is left out of the picture. Simon Fish, an Oxford student who entered Gray's Inn
about 1525, joined a circle of young men in London who
were very critical of Cardinal Thomas Wolsey, King Henry
VIII's chief minister, and the hierarchy. As a chauvinistic anti-
clerical pamphleteer, he helped to stir up feeling among the
rabble against the churchmen with his *Supplication of Beggars* which he circulated in the city as early as 1529. Fish was
embittered when he was forced into exile following a quarrel
with Cardinal Wolsey, and he was later instrumental in dis-
tributing copies of the Protestant William Tyndale's New
Testament. John Fox in his *Acts and Monuments* relates that
Anne Boleyn, King Henry VIII's second wife, gave a copy of
the Supplication to her husband. Henry then asked to meet
the author, who was in hiding nearby. The King embraced
him, took him hunting with him, and gave him the royal
signet to protect him from Chancellor Thomas More, the
staunch defender of the Catholic faith. Fish died of the plague
the next year in 1531. From Frederick J. Furnivall, ed., *A
Supplication for the Beggars, Written about the Year 1529 by
Simon Fish* (London: N. Trübner & Co., 1871), pp. 1-15, spelling modernized.

To the King our Sovereign Lord

Most lamentably complaineth their woeful misery unto Your Highness, your poor daily bedesmen, the wretched hideous monsters (on whom scarcely for horror any of you dare look), the foul unhappy sort of lepers and other sore people, needy, impotent, blind, lame and sick, that live only by alms; how that their number is daily so sore increased that all the alms of all well-disposed people of this your realm is not half enough for to sustain them, but that for very constraint they die for hunger. And this most pestilent mischief is come upon your said poor bedesmen, by the reason that there is in the time of your noble predecessors passed craftily crept into this your realm another sort (not of impotent but) of strong, puissant and counterfeit holy and idle beggars and vagabonds, which since the time of their first entry by all the craft and wiliness of Satan are now increased under your sight not only into a great number, but also into a kingdom. These are (not the herds, but the ravenous wolves going in herds' clothing devouring the flock) the bishops, abbots, priors, deacons, archdeacons, suffragans, priests, monks, canons, friars, pardoners and summoners. And who is able to number this idle ravenous sort, which (setting all labor aside) have begged so importunately that they have gotten into their hands more than the third part of all your realm? The goodliest lordships, manors, lands and territories are theirs. Besides this they have the tenth part of all the corn, meadow, pasture, grass, wool, colts, calves, lambs, pigs, geese and chickens. Over and besides, the tenth part of every servant's wages [and] the tenth part of the wool, milk, honey, wax, cheese and butter. Yes, and they look so narrowly upon their profits that the poor wives must be accountable to them of every tenth egg or else she gets not her rights at Easter [and] shall be taken as a heretic. Hereto have they their four offering days. What money pull they in by probates of testaments, privy tithes, and by men's offerings to their pilgrimages, and at their first masses? Every man and child that is buried must pay somewhat for masses and dirges to be sung for him or else they will accuse the dead's friends and executors of heresy. What money get they by mortuaries, by hearing of confessions (and yet they will keep thereof no counsel), by hallowing of churches, altars, superaltars, chapels and bells, by cursing of men and absolving them again for money? What a multitude of money gather the pardoners in a year? How much money get the summoners by extortion in a year, by citing the people to the commissary's court and afterward releasing their appearance for money? Finally, the infinite number of begging friars, what get they in a year? Here, if it please your grace to mark, you shall see a thing far out of joint. . . . Oh grievous and painful exactions thus yearly to be paid, from the which the people of your noble predecessors, the kings of the ancient Britons, ever stood free! And this will they have or else they will procure him that will not give it them to be taken as an heretic. What tyrant ever oppressed the people like this cruel and vengeful generation? What subjects shall be able to help their prince that be after this fashion yearly polled? What good Christian people can be able to succor us poor lepers, blind, sore and lame, that be thus yearly oppressed? Is it any marvel that your people so complain of poverty? Is it any marvel that the taxes, fifteens and subsidies that your grace most tenderly of great compassion hath taken among your people to defend them from the threatened ruin of their commonwealth, have been so slothfully, yes, painfully levied? Seeing that almost the utmost penny that might have been levied hath been gathered before yearly by this ravenous, cruel and insatiable generation. . . .

Yes, and what do they more? Truly nothing but apply themselves by all the slights they may have to do with every man's wife, every man's daughter, and every man's maid, that cuckoldry and bawdry should reign over all among your subjects, that no man should know his own child, that their bastards might inherit the possessions of every man to put the right begotten children clear beside their inheritance in subversion of all estates and godly order. These be they that by their abstaining from marriage do [prevent] the generation of the people, whereby all the realm at length, if it should be continued, shall be made desert and unhabitable. . . . Oh, the grievous shipwreck of the commonwealth, which in ancient time before the coming in of these ravenous wolves was so prosperous. . . .

Set these sturdy loobies abroad in the world to get them wives of their own, to get their living with their labor in the sweat of their faces, according to the commandment of God, Genesis 3, to give other idle people by their example occasion to go to labor. Tie these holy idle thieves to the carts, to be whipped naked about every market town until they will fall to labor; that they, by their importunate begging take not away the alms that the good Christian people would give unto us sore, impotent, miserable people, your bedesmen. Then shall as well the number of our aforesaid monstrous sort, as of the bawds, whores, thieves and idle people decrease. Then shall these great yearly enactions cease. Then shall not your sword, power, crown, dignity and obedience of your people be translated from you. Then shall you have full obedience of your people. Then shall the idle people be set to work. Then shall matrimony be much better kept. Then shall your commons increase in riches. Then shall the gospel be preached. Then shall none beg our alms from us. Then shall we have enough and more than shall suffice us, which shall be the best hospital that ever was founded for us. Then shall we daily pray to God for your most noble estate long to endure.

2. Cromwell: The Restraint of Appeals to Rome, 1533

The man who laid down the legal bases of the English national church was Thomas Cromwell (1485?-1540), who in 1530 succeeded Cardinal Thomas Wolsey (1471-1530) as King Henry VIII's chief minister after his fall. From 1532 until his own destruction in 1540 he determined to a large extent the royal policy toward the Church. Cromwell had experience in an Italian business firm and had the tastes of a Renaissance personality. He devoted himself to the King, promoted the theory of royal supremacy, and insisted upon the submission of the clergy to the crown. The preamble to the Act of Parliament for *The Restraint of Appeals to Rome*, 1533, which Cromwell drafted, reveals his ideas about the place of the church in the realm where King cooperated with the people represented in Parliament. From Henry Gee and William Hardy, eds., *Documents Illustrative of English Church History* (London: Macmillan and Co., Ltd., 1896), pp. 187-192.

Where by divers sundry old authentic histories and chronicles it is manifestly declared and expressed that this realm of England is an empire, and so hath been accepted in the world; governed by one supreme head and king, having the dignity and royal estate of the imperial crown of the same; unto whom a body politic, compact of all sorts and degrees of people, divided in terms and by names of spirituality and temporalty, be bounden and ought to bear, next to God, a natural and humble obedience: he being also institute and furnished by the goodness and sufferance of Almighty God with plenary, whole, and entire power, pre-eminence, authority, prerogative and jurisdiction, to render and yield justice and final determination to all manner of folk, residents, or subjects within this his realm, in all causes, matters, debates and contentions happening to occur, insurge or begin within the limits thereof, without restraint or provocation to any foreign princes or potentates of the world; the body spiritual whereof having power, when any cause of the law divine or of spiritual learning happened to come in question, then it was declared, interpreted, and showed by that part of the said body politic called the spirituality, now being usually called the English Church, which always hath been reputed, and also found of that sort, that both for knowledge, integrity, and sufficiency of number, it hath been always thought, and is also at this hour, sufficient and meet of itself, without the intermeddling of any exterior person or persons, to declare and determine all such doubts and to administer all such offices and duties as to their rooms spiritual doth appertain; for the due administration whereof, and to keep them from corruption and sinister affection, the king's most noble progenitors and the antecessors of the nobles of this realm have sufficiently endowed the said Church both with honor and possessions; and the laws temporal, for trial of property of lands and goods, and for the conservation of the people of this realm in unity and peace, without ravin or spoil, was and yet is administered, adjudged and executed by sundry judges and ministers of the other part of the said body politic called the temporalty; and both their authorities and jurisdictions do conjoin together in the due administration of justice, the one to help the other.

And whereas the king, his most noble progenitors and the nobility and Commons of this said realm, at divers and sundry parliaments, as well in the time of King Edward I, Edward III,

Richard II, Henry IV and other noble kings of this realm, made sundry ordinances, laws, statutes and provisions for the entire and sure conservation of the prerogatives, liberties and pre-eminences of the said imperial crown of this realm, and of the jurisdiction spiritual and temporal of the same, to keep it from the annoyance as well of the see of Rome as from the authority of other foreign potentates, attempting the diminution or violation thereof, as often, and from time to time, as any such annoyance or attempt might be known or espied.

And notwithstanding the said good statutes and ordinances made in the time of the king's most noble progenitors of the said imperial crown, as is aforesaid; yet nevertheless since the making of the said good statues and ordinances, divers and sundry inconveniences and dangers not provided for plainly by the said former acts, statutes and ordinances have arisen and sprung by reason of appeals sued out of this realm to the sea of Rome, in causes testamentary, causes of matrimony and divorces, right of tithes, oblations and obventions, not only to the great inquietation, vexation, trouble, cost and charges of the king's highness and many of his subjects and residents in this his realm, but also to the great delay and let to the true and speedy determination of the said causes; for so much as the parties appealing to the said Court of Rome most commonly do the same for the delay of justice.

And forasmuch as the great distance of way is so far out of this realm, so that [neither] the necessary proofs nor the true knowledge of the cause, can . . . be so well known, nor the witnesses there so well examined, as within this realm, so that the parties grieved by means of the said appeals be most times without remedy:

In consideration whereof the king's highness, his nobles and Commons, considering the great enormities, dangers, long delays and hurts that do daily ensue as well to his highness as to his said nobles, subjects, commons and residents of this his realm, in the said causes testamentary, causes of matrimony and divorces, tithes, oblations and obventions; does therefore by his royal assent, and by the assent of the lords spiritual and temporal and the Commons in this present Parliament assembled, and by authority of the same, enact, establish and ordain that all causes testamentary, causes of matrimony and divorces, rights of tithes, oblations and obventions (the knowledge whereof by the goodness of princes of

this realm, and by the laws and customs of the same, appertaineth
to the spiritual jurisdiction of this realm) already commenced,
moved, depending, being, happening, or hereafter coming in contention, debate or question within this realm or within any [of]
the king's dominions or marches of the same, or elsewhere, whether
they concern the king our sovereign lord, his heirs and successors,
or any other subjects or residents within the same, of what degree
soever they be, shall be from henceforth heard, examined, discussed, clearly, finally and definitely adjudged and determined
within the king's jurisdiction and authority, and not elsewhere, in
such courts spiritual and temporal of the same, as the natures,
conditions and qualities of the causes and matters aforesaid in
contention, or hereafter happening in contention, shall require;
without having any respect to any custom, use, or sufferance, in
hindrance, let, or prejudice of the same, or to any other thing used
or suffered to the contrary thereof by any other manner of person
or persons in any manner [or] wise: any foreign inhibitions, appeals, sentences, summons, citations, suspensions, interdictions,
excommunications, restraints, judgments, or any other process or
impediments, of what natures, names, qualities or conditions soever they be, from the see of Rome or any other foreign courts
or potentates of the world, or from and out of this realm or any
other [of] the king's dominions or marches of the same, to the see
of Rome or to any other foreign courts or potentates, to the let
[hindrance] or impediment thereof in any wise notwithstanding.

And that it shall be lawful to the king our sovereign lord, and
to his heirs and successors, and to all other subjects or residents
within this realm, or within any [of] the king's dominions or
marches of the same—notwithstanding that hereafter . . . should
happen any excommengement, excommunications, interdictions,
citations, or any other censures or foreign process out of any outward parts, to be fulminated, provulged, declared, or put in execution within this said realm, or in any other place or places, for
any of the causes before rehearsed, in prejudice, derogation, or
contempt of this said Act and the very true meaning and execution thereof—may and shall nevertheless as. well pursue, execute,
have and enjoy the effects, profits, benefits and commodities of
all such processes, sentences, judgments and determinations done,
or hereafter to be done, in any of the said courts spiritual or temporal, as the cases shall require, within the limits, power and

authority of this the king's said realm, and dominions and marches of the same, and those only, and none other to take place, and to be firmly observed and obeyed within the same.

As also, that all the spiritual prelates, pastors, ministers and curates within this realm and the dominions of the same shall and may use, minister, execute and do, or cause to be used, ministered, executed and done, all sacraments, sacramentals, divine services and all other things within the said realm and dominions, unto all the subjects of the same, as catholic and Christian men ought to do; any former citations, processes, inhibitions, suspensions, interdictions, excommunications or appeals, for or touching the causes aforesaid, from or to the see of Rome or any other foreign prince or foreign courts, to the let [hindrance] or contrary thereof in any wise notwithstanding.

And if any of the said spiritual persons, by the occasion of the said fulminations of any of the same interdictions, censures, inhibitions, excommunications, appeals, suspensions, summons, or other foreign citations for the causes beforesaid, or for any of them, do at any time hereafter refuse to minister, or cause to be ministered, the said sacraments and sacramentals and other divine services, in form as is aforesaid, shall for every such time or times that they or any of them do refuse so to do, or cause to be done, have one year's imprisonment, and [shall pay] fine and ransom at the king's pleasure.

And it is further enacted by the authority aforesaid, that if any person or persons inhabiting or resident within this realm, or within any of the king's said dominions, or marches of the same, or any other person or persons, of what estate, condition, or degree soever he or they be, at any time hereafter, for or in any the causes aforesaid, do attempt, move, purchase or procure, from or to the see of Rome, or from or to any other foreign court or courts out of this realm, any manner [of] foreign process, inhibitions, appeals, sentences, summons, citations, suspensions, interdictions, excommunications, restraints or judgments, of whatsoever nature, kind or quality they be, or execute any of the same process, or do any act or acts to the let, impediment, hindrance or derogation of any process, sentence, judgment or determination had, made, done, or hereafter to be had, done or made, in any courts of this realm, or the king's said dominions or marches of the same, for any of the causes aforesaid, contrary to the true meaning of this present Act and the execution of the same, that then every such person or persons so doing, and their fautors [patrons], comforters, abettors, procurers, executors and counsellors, and every [one] of them, being convicted of the same, for every such default shall incur and run in the same pains, penalties and forfeitures ordained and provided by the Statute of Provision and Praemunire, made in the sixteenth year of the reign of the right noble prince King Richard II, against such as attempt, procure, or make provision to the see of Rome, or elsewhere, for any thing or things, to the derogation [of] or contrary to the prerogative or jurisdiction of the crown and dignity of this realm.

3. Starkey: Exhortation to Unity and Obedience

Among the publicists who promoted Cromwell's policies and commended them to the people was Thomas Starkey (1499?-1538), a young humanist who had enjoyed the patronage of Cardinal Reginald Pole in Italy, but had returned to serve the King. As chaplain to Henry VIII he wrote in 1535 the remarkable *Exhortation to the People Instructing Them to Unity and Obedience*, the earliest expression of the *via media* and a plea for moderation characteristic of Anglicanism. Drawing upon the conciliar theories of Marsiglio of Padua, upon arguments from natural reason and natural law, and upon the Scriptures, and inspired by the moderate Lutheranism of Melanchthon, who wrote of *adiaphora* or things indifferent to salvation, Starkey in the *Exhortation* urged the people to shun extremes and violence, to find a midway between papism and radicalism, and to preserve unity and obedience in all Christian charity. The following passages are taken from the address to the readers in the edition of 1536 by the king's printer Thomas Berthelet, spelling modernized.

An exhortation to the people instructing them to unity and obedience.

As it is to all other creatures by the power of God brought forth into this world naturally given by His goodness to desire their end and perfection, the which they be ordained unto, so it is to the nature of man, who of all others here in earth is most noble and of dignity most excellent, as he that is with reason endowed—the most heavenly thing—whereof bodily creatures and earthly may be partakers, by the which as by the chief instrument he may seek and insearch all convenient means whereby he may attain the better to such end and perfection as by the goodness of God to him is appointed. And although this desire be to all mankind common, and ever has been of what religion soever they be, yet we most Christian people, which be of Christ's flock and lighted with the Spirit of God make profession of His name, above all other ought to be thereof most desirous, as they which have by the singular benefit of God a more sure knowledge and a more sure ground to lean unto than any other people in earth; for we have the express and manifest doctrine of God by the which we are taught and instructed [in] the straight and sure way to the attaining of our felicity, the which stands neither in worldly honor, pleasure, nor high dignity, . . . nor yet in any secret knowledge of subtle philosophy. For then it should not be common but to few, and the multitude of Christian people should be excluded from it. But according to the whole course of the doctrine of our most loving master Christ, it rests only in faithful love and charitable unity. . . .

For because I have here following somewhat more briefly than the nature of the thing doth well suffer comprised and gathered unto the people a certain instruction whereby they might the better be induced to such unity and obedience as is of them most justly required, I shall, most Christian readers, here in this prologue open unto you a little more at large what is the nature of this obedience and unity to the which we be so straightly bound both by God's law and all good civility, and touch also somewhat the cause which has chiefly moved me to the conceiving of this matter and purpose. But here in the beginning, to the intent the thing may the better be perceived, I do require you a little to lift up your eyes with some consideration, to weigh with yourself in some part the divine power, wisdom and providence, though the thing fully to conceive far surmounts all man's wit and imagination.

And first this is open and manifest that all this sensible world wherein is contained this wonderful variety and nature of things is nothing else but as a certain shadow of God's goodness and divinity, or rather a glass of the divine majesty, whereby to man's judgment and capacity is opened the infinite power and wonderful wisdom of Him Who by His high providence governs and rules all. For whithersoever you cast your eyes, either above unto heaven—there beholding that heavenly body in his sincerity, [or] here beneath unto the earth—there considering of nature the wonderful variety, you shall ever see of that power and providence in everything most certain argument and sure testimony. Whereof I think no man can doubt, who with any consideration looking into this glass, there stands in marvel and admiration. . . .

Whereas many men nowadays, considering the state of the Christian policy vexed with so much sedition and heresy, fear much to see shortly great ruin and decay thereof, I would have them to alter that opinion and to stand fully in this persuasion, that this division by sects and contrary opinion reigning among Christian nations the goodness of God shall turn to His honor and glory and to the setting forth of His true religion, the which long and many a day has been by simple superstition much obscured and hid; yes, and though it were so that in foolishly fleeing this superstition we should a while slip into the contrary, that is to say, the contempt of religion, yet I doubt not but the goodness of God in time convenient would reduce us at the last to the mean and bring unto light the knowledge of His true religion, as He hath done in all times from the beginning of the world unto this day, by little and little ever drawing man's weakness to the true way. And this manner with us I doubt not but that His goodness will us now in these days so inspire and give light to the hearts of His Christian flock that they all with concord and unity shall to His will be obedient most meekly. This hope and trust I have fixed in my heart, wherewith I much comfort myself. And though there be here in our nation growing in a certain division, by corrupt judgement and false opinion, yet I trust we shall not so far slip from God's providence that it may take among us any such root whereby shall spring any sedition or of good and civil order any ruin or destruction. But contrary, if we as members of one body run all together after one fashion, I trust at length surely it shall minister a great occasion to the setting forth of Christ's true religion. For the which cause now I have conceived this little instruction, exhorting our people to unity and obedience, the lack whereof in the state of Christen-

dom has been a great cause of much division, and especially in the
country of Germany, where as by the foolish avoiding of superstition they have slipped into great discord and sedition, whose example I trust shall be to us a spectacle, ministering unto us no small
instruction. Especially if we consider groundly the cause and foundation of all their controversy and sedition, the which doubtless
rose of things in no point necessary to man's salvation, but about
ceremonies and traditions to the which many men blinded by superstition leaned none otherwise than to Christ's word and gospel.
They did not discern with right judgement betwixt things of themselves good and necessary and other, which are only for the time
convenient to a certain policy, but all things of long time received
by custom and general decree, some of them taken as God's law
indifferently and some all turned up so done indiscretely. Wherefore such persons as by the examination of them to God's word
found therein much abuse, first the rest could not well bear, but
noted them [as heretics] and as movers of sedition. By the reason
whereof sprang the great division whereby the country was divided into many and divers sects; but now by the providence of
God, each one spying the folly of other, they begin to fall unto the
mean, that is to say, to Christ's true religion, giving to God's word
the full authority, that [of] preaching without abrogation. And as
for ceremonies and traditions, they suffer as things convenient to
maintain unity, whereas they repugn neither to God's word nor to
good civility. The which thing, if they had done at the beginning,
they should not by their blindness have fallen to such confusion,
nor by their foolish correction of the abuses of the church have
brought in such a division. Howbeit I doubt not but that the
providence of God has suffered this thing for the institution of
other, for we may, as I often rehearse, take example of that folly
and run together in one course with obedience and unity. The
which, if we do, we shall doubtless shortly see the providence of
God so work that out of our church and congregation we shall see
plucked up all superstitious abuses. [On the other hand], if we
proceed in our corrupt judgement and . . . in [our recent] division, we shall without fail slip to like confusion. For the avoiding whereof I· have directed to the people this rude instruction,
moving them to obedience and unity. . . .

Here in this place somewhat I will touch both how you shall
come unto the true sense of God's word and also what obedience

you ought for to give both to general council and princes' authority. And first this you shall understand as a sure ground to the resolution hereof that such things to . . . which we owe our obedience and [to which we] are bounden unto either by God's word, general council, or princes' authority, be of four sorts and of three diverse kinds. For either they be of their own nature good and profitable or, contrary, by nature ill and damnable, or else indifferent, which of [itself] be neither good nor ill. As by an example, such things are good, not as appears to man's corrupt reason, but such as be by God's own word defined, by the which rule only we must examine what thing is good with right judgement, as to trust in God and in His only goodness, to love Him above all things, and thy brother as thyself; these with such other expressed by God's word are by nature good and profitable. As contrary, such things as by the same word are prohibited and forbidden are by nature ill and damnable, as to distrust the mercy of God and doubt of His goodness, to have thy brother in hate, or wrongfully to covet worldly riches.

Things indifferent I call all such things which by God's word are neither prohibited nor commanded, but left to worldly policy, whereof they take their full authority, by the which as time and place requires, they are sometimes good and sometimes ill. As to eat flesh [on] Friday and after the customed manner to keep the Holy Day, to go a pilgrimage and pray unto saints, these and other like I call things indifferent, and nothing necessary to man's salvation, though they may be well used and after a good fashion, as I shall hereafter more at large open and declare. Among the which also I number this great matter of the pope's superiority, which so troubles many weak consciences. For as I judge it not so ill and damnable that all our forefathers which have been obedient thereto this seven hundred years therefore be damned, so I judge it not so good that obedience thereto shall be necessary to them which should be saved, as I have at large declared in the matter following, and opened therein fully my opinion. But now to the purpose: this and all other like which be not in Scripture expressed by commandment I note to be things indifferent, the nature of whom is of this sort, which is highly here to be observed; that though of themselves, they be neither good nor ill, nor to them we owe no obedience, yet when they be set out with authority by them which have whole rule in any kind of policy, whether it be in the state, of a prince, or popular, then the people are to them bound; yes, by the virtue of God's own Word, who commanded expressly His disciples to be obedient to common policy whensoever thereby is commanded anything which is not repugnant to His precepts and doctrine, yes, and though it were contrary to their own private profit, pleasure and quietness, yes, or contrary to a worldly right-wiseness. Yet would He have His disciples and the professors of His name ever to be obedient with humility and meekness, where-with as with a peculiar mark He hath marked his flock. . . .

For as to pride and arrogance Christ ever resists, so to lowliness and humility His grace ever He communes. That He exalts and sets in high dignity, even as pride He ever depresses and puts under foot. So that by this gate we must enter, which few men find, if we will follow Him and to the mysteries of His doctrine take the true way. For except we be as children lowly and meek without all cor-rupt affection, there shall to us be no gate open to bring us to His kingdom and heavenly perfection. This is the true trace wherein he must tread, whosoever fruitfully will seek the true sense of God's Word. [And he] who so entereth doubtless shall find, to such scruple of conscience, a singular remedy without further expectation of general council and decree. And never shall [he] fear to give obedi-ence to such things as be decreed by common authority, especially seeing they touch only things indifferent, nothing necessary to our salvation; as I think it shall be evident unto all . . . who will thoroughly read and indifferently weigh such things as I have gathered in this little instruction. And then I shall not doubt but that we shall run all together in one course in Christian unity, which shortly to touch stands in this point chiefly.

We must conceive, if we will be true professors of Christ's doc-trine, a certain brotherly love each one toward other, judging our-selves to be born of one Father, nourished of one mother, members of one body, hanging of one head, looking for one reward promised to us, living together in this unity. We must think that our master Christ descended down from the bosom of His Father to establish this concord and unity in the hearts of all them which purpose to be inheritors with Him in the kingdom of heaven everlastingly. We must think that by this only is the way to immortality, the which, if we do, I doubt not; but that all such division as hangs

over our heads, which might bring . . . confusion into this our
country and policy, we shall right well avoid and eschew, living
together in due obedience and perfect unity. For the which I shall
not cease to pray unto Him who hath promised surely to give the
light of truth to all them which demand it meekly, and the same
shall require of you all to whom it shall chance to read this instruction. And of this to make a sure conclusion, that if we with meekness and humility, faithful love and charity, seek out the true sense
of God's word diligently, we shall surely find it and such light
thereof receive that though we never hear of pope nor cardinal,
nor yet of council general, yet shall we not be destitute of such
truth and light as is necessary to our salvation. But here I will make
an end and trouble you with no longer preface, remitting you to
the instruction for further declaration.

4. Henry VIII: The Six Articles, 1539

The basically conservative position of King Henry VIII himself on doctrinal matters is evident from the Six Articles Act
which was passed by Parliament in June, 1539, upon the initia-
tive and authority of the King as well as in his presence. The
Articles reaffirmed six basic Catholic doctrines and were called
by Protestants the "bloody whip with six strings." They were
opposed by Thomas Cranmer, Archbishop of Canterbury, who
was, however, forced to submit. From Henry Gee and William
Hardy, eds., *Documents Illustrative of English Church History*
(London: Macmillan and Co., Ltd., 1896), pp. 304-306.

The king's most royal majesty, most prudently ponder-
ing and considering that by occasion of variable and sundry opinions and judgments of the said Articles great discord and variance
has arisen, as well amongst the clergy of this his realm as amongst
a great number of vulgar people, his loving subjects of the same;
and being in a full hope and trust that a full and perfect resolution
of the said Articles should make a perfect concord and unity gen-

erally amongst all his loving and obedient subjects of his most excellent goodness; not only commanded that the said Articles should deliberately and advisedly, by his said archbishops, bishops and other learned men of his clergy, be debated, argued and reasoned, and their opinions therein to be understood, declared and known, but also most graciously vouchsafed, in his own princely person, to descend and come into his said High Court of Parliament and council, and there, like a prince of most high prudence and no less learning, opened and declared many things of high learning and great knowledge touching the said Articles, matters and questions for a unity to be had in the same; whereupon, after a great and long, deliberate and advised disputation and consultation had and made concerning the said Articles, as well by the consent of the king's highness as by the assent of the lords spiritual and temporal and other learned men of his clergy in their Convocation, and by the consent of the Commons in this present Parliament assembled, it was and is finally resolved, accorded and agreed in manner and form following, that is to say:

First, that in the most blessed Sacrament of the altar, by the strength and efficacy of Christ's mighty word (it being spoken by the priest), is present really, under the form of bread and wine, the natural body and blood of our Saviour Jesus Christ, conceived of the Virgin Mary; and that after the consecration there remaineth no substance of bread or wine, nor any other substance, but the substance of Christ, God and man.

Secondly, that communion in both kinds is not necessary *ad salutem*, by the law of God, to all persons; and that it is to be believed and not doubted of, but that in the flesh, under the form of bread, is the very blood; and with the blood, under the form of wine, is the very flesh; as well apart as though they were both together.

Thirdly, that priests after the order of priesthood received, as afore, may not marry, by the law of God.

Fourthly, that vows of chastity or widowhood, by man or woman made to God advisedly, ought to be observed by the law of God; and that it exempts them from other liberties of Christian people, which without that they might enjoy.

Fifthly, that it is meet and necessary that private masses be continued and admitted in this the king's English Church and congregation, as whereby good Christian people, ordering themselves accordingly, do receive both godly and goodly consolations and benefits; and it is agreeable also to God's law.

Sixthly, that auricular confession is expedient and necessary to be retained and continued, used and frequented in the Church of God.

5. Cranmer: Preface to the Bible

The Archbishop of Canterbury Thomas Cranmer (1489-1556), faithful and loyal to the crown, was a key figure in the intro-duction of the Reformation in England not merely as the Primate of all England and church administration, but also as a learned theologian and religious leader. Influenced both by the Continental reformers and by extensive reading in the early Church fathers, Cranmer emphasized the importance of the Scriptures as the source of Christian teaching and derived from them his understanding of justification by faith, the all-sufficiency of God's grace, and the real presence of Christ in the Sacrament. In April, 1540, Cranmer's *Prologue or Preface to the Bible* was prefixed to the great Bible appointed to be read in the churches, properly called Cranmer's Bible, imple-menting the Protestant principle of *sola scriptura* and the con-cept of the priesthood of all believers. From the *Miscellaneous Writings and Letters of Thomas Cranmer,* edited for the Parker Society (Cambridge: The University Press, 1846), pp. 118-125.

A PROLOGUE OR PREFACE
made by The Most Reverend Father in God

THOMAS, ARCHBISHOP OF CANTERBURY
Metropolitan and Primate of England

For two sundry sorts of people it seemeth much necessary that something be said in the entry of this book, by the way of a preface or prologue; whereby hereafter it may be both the better accepted of them which hitherto could not well bear it, and also the better used of them which heretofore have misused it. For truly some there are that be too slow and need the spur; some other seem too quick and need more of the bridle; some lose their game by short shooting, some by overshooting; some walk too much on the left hand, some too much on the right. In the former sort be all they that refuse to read, or to hear read the Scripture in the vulgar tongues; much worse they that also let [hinder] or discourage the other from the reading or hearing thereof. In the latter sort be they which, by their inordinate reading, indiscreet speaking, contentious disputing, or otherwise by their licentious living, slander and hinder the Word of God most of all other, whereof they would seem to be [its] greatest furtherers. These two sorts, albeit they be most far unlike the one to the other, yet they both deserve in effect like reproach. Neither can I well tell [which] of them I may judge the [greater] offender, him that doth obstinately refuse so godly and goodly knowledge, or him that so ungodly and so ungoodly doth abuse the same.

And as touching the former, I would marvel much that any man should be so mad as to refuse in darkness, light; in hunger, food; in cold, fire. For the Word of God is light—*lucerna pedibus meis verbum tuum;* food—*non in solo pane vivit homo, sed in omni verbo Dei;* fire—*ignem veni mittere in terram, et quid volo, nisit ut ardeat?* I would marvel (I say) at this, save that I consider how much custom and usage may do. So that if there were a people, as some write, *De Cimmeriis,* which never saw the sun by reason that they be situated far toward the north pole and be inclosed and over-shadowed with high mountains, it is credible and like enough that if, by the power and will of God, the mountains should sink down and give place [and] the light of the sun might have entrance to them, at the first some of them would be offended therewith. And the old proverb affirmeth that, after tillage of corn was first found, many delighted more to feed of mast and acorns, wherewith they had been accustomed, than to eat bread made of good corn. Such is the nature of custom that it causeth us to bear all things well and easily wherewith we have been accustomed, and to be offended with all things thereunto contrary. And therefore I can well think them worthy pardon which, at the coming abroad of Scripture, doubted and drew back. But such as will persist still in their willfulness, I must needs judge not only foolish, forward and obstinate, but also peevish, perverse and indurate.

And yet, if the matter should be tried by custom, we might also allege custom for the reading of the Scripture in the vulgar tongues, and prescribe the more ancient custom. For it is not much above one hundred years . . . since Scripture hath not been accustomed to be read in the vulgar tongues within this realm; and many hundred years before that it was translated and read in the Saxons' tongue, which at that time was our mother tongue; whereof there remaineth yet divers copies found lately in old abbeys, of such antique manners of writing and speaking that few men now [are] able to read and understand them. And when this language waxed old and out of common usage, [so that] folk should not lack the fruit of reading, it was again translated in the newer language. Whereof yet also many copies remain and be daily found.

But now to . . . pass [on from] custom, and to weigh, as wise men ever should, the thing in [its] own nature: let us here discuss what availeth Scripture to be had and read [by] the lay and vulgar people. And to this question I intend here to say nothing but that was spoken and written by the noble doctor and most moral divine, St. John Chrysostom [a Greek church father of Antioch and Constantinople, 340-407], in his third sermon *De Lazaro*; albeit I will be something shorter and gather the matter into fewer words and less room than he doth there, because I would not be tedious. He exhorteth there his audience that every man should read by himself at home in the mean days and time, between sermon and sermon, to the intent they might both more profoundly fix in their minds and memories that he had said before upon such texts, whereupon he had already preached; and also that they might have their minds the more ready and better prepared to receive and perceive that which he should say from thenceforth in his sermons, upon such texts as he had not yet declared and preached upon. . . .

Hitherto, all that I have said I have taken and gathered out of the aforesaid sermon of this holy doctor, St. John Chrysostom. Now if I should in like manner bring forth what the selfsame doctor speaketh in other places, and what other doctors and writers say concerning the same purpose, I might seem to you to write another bible rather than to make a preface to the Bible. Wherefore, in few words [we] comprehend the largeness and utility of the Scripture, how it containeth fruitful instruction and erudition for every man; [how] if anything be necessary to be learned, of the holy Scripture we may learn it. If falsehood shall be reproved, thereof we may gather wherewithal. If anything be to be corrected and amended, if there need any exhortation or consolation, of the Scripture we may well learn. In the Scriptures be the fat pastures of the soul; therein is no venomous meat, no unwholesome thing; they be the very dainty and pure feeding. He that is ignorant shall find there what he should learn. He that is a perverse sinner shall there find his damnation to make him to tremble for fear. He that laboreth to serve God shall find there his glory and the promises of eternal life, exhorting him more diligently to labor. Herein may princes learn how to govern their subjects; subjects obedience, love and dread to their princes; husbands how they should behave them unto their wives [and] how to educate their children and servants; and contrary the wives, children and servants may know their duty to their husbands, parents and masters. Here . . . all manner of persons—men, women, young, old, learned, unlearned, rich, poor, priests, laymen, lords, ladies, officers, tenants and mean men, virgins, wives, widows, lawyers, merchants, artificers, husbandmen and all manner of persons, of what estate or condition soever they be—may in this book learn . . . what they ought to believe, what they ought to do and what they should not do, as well concerning Almighty God as also concerning themselves and all other. Briefly, to the reading of the Scripture none can be enemy, but that either be so sick that they love not to hear of any medicine, or else that be so ignorant that they know not Scripture to be the most healthful medicine. Therefore, as touching this former part, I will here conclude and take it as a conclusion sufficiently determined and approved, that it is convenient and good [for] the Scripture to be read [by] all sorts and kinds of people, and in the vulgar tongue, without further allegations and probations for the same; which shall not need, since that this one place of John Chrysostom is enough and sufficient to persuade all them that be not frowardly and perversely set in their own willful opinion; specially now that the king's highness, being supreme head next under Christ of this church of England, hath approved with his royal assent the setting forth hereof, which only to all true and obedient subjects ought to be a sufficient reason for the allowance of the same, without further delay, reclamation or resistance, although there were no preface nor other reason herein expressed.

Therefore now to come to the second and latter part of my purpose. There is nothing so good in this world but it may be abused and turned from fruitful and wholesome to hurtful and noisome. What is there above better than the sun, the moon, the stars? Yet was [were] there [those] that took occasion by the great beauty and virtue of them to dishonor God and to defile themselves with idolatry, giving the honor of the living God and Creator of all things to such things as He had created. What is there here beneath better than fire, water, meats, drinks, metals of gold, silver, iron and steel? Yet we see daily great harm and much mischief done by every one of these, as well for lack of wisdom and providence of them that suffer evil, as by the malice of them that worketh the evil. Thus to them that be evil of themselves everything setteth forward and increaseth their evil, be it of [its] own nature a thing never so good; like as contrarily, to them that studieth and endeavoreth themselves to goodness, everything prevaileth them and profiteth unto good, be it of [its] own nature a thing never so bad. As St. Paul saith: *His qui diligant Deum, omnia cooperantur in bonum:* even as out of most venomous worms is made treacle, the most sovereign medicine for the preservation of man's health in time of danger. Wherefore I would advise you all that cometh to the reading or hearing of this book, which is the Word of God, the most precious jewel and most holy relic that remaineth upon earth, that ye bring with you the fear of God, and that ye do it with all due reverence, and use your knowledge thereof not to vainglory [or] frivolous disputation but to the honor of God, increase of virtue and edification both of yourselves and other. . . .

Therefore to conclude this latter part, every man that cometh to the reading of this holy book ought to bring with him first and foremost this fear of Almighty God, and then next a firm and stable purpose to reform his own self according thereunto; and so to continue, proceed, and prosper from time to time, showing himself to be a sober and fruitful hearer and learner. Which if he do, he shall prove at the length well able to teach, though not with his mouth yet with his living and good example, which is surely the most lively and most effectual form and manner of teaching. He that otherwise intermeddleth with this book, let him be assured that once he shall make account therefore, when he shall have said to him, as it is written in the prophet David, *Peccatori dicit Deus, etc.* [Ps. 50, 16-23]: "Unto the ungodly said God, 'Why dost thou preach my laws, and takest my testament in thy mouth? Whereas thou hatest to be reformed, and hast been partakers with advoutrers [adulterers]. Thou hast let thy mouth speak wickedness, and with thy tongue thou hast set forth deceit. Thou sattest and spakest against thy brother; and hast slandered thine own mother's son. These things hast thou done, and I held my tongue, and thou thoughtest (wickedly) that I am even such a one as thyself. But I will reprove thee, and set before thee the things that thou hast done. O consider this, ye that forget God; lest I pluck you away, and there be none to deliver you. Whoso offereth me thanks and praise, he honoreth me; and to him that ordereth his conversation right will I show the salvation of God.' "

God save the King.

6. Lady Jane Grey: A Certain Communication

During King Edward's final years the Duke of Northumberland dominated his government. Fearing the accession of Mary and determined to maintain his power, the Duke organized a conspiracy to subvert the succession, exclude Mary, and secure the crown for Lady Jane Grey, the daughter of Henry VIII's niece. The Duke married his son to Lady Jane Grey and hoped thus to perpetuate himself in power. The plot failed when the English rallied to Mary, 'a true Tudor, and poor Lady Jane was imprisoned. Four days before she was beheaded this sixteen-year-old girl wrote out her dialogue with a Master Feckenham which reveals her understanding of Christian thelogy in Protestant terms. From the *Harleian Miscellany*, I (London: Printed for R. Dutton, 1808), pp. 369-371, spelling modernized.

A certain communication between the Lady Jane and Master Feckenham, four days before her death, even word for word, her own hand being put thereto.

Feckenham speaks first.

What thing is required in a Christian?

Jane: To believe in God the Father, in God the Son, in God the Holy Ghost, three persons and one God.

Feckenham: Is there nothing else required in a Christian but to believe in God?

Jane: Yes, we must believe in Him, we must love Him with all our heart, with all our soul and all our mind, and our neighbor as ourself.

Feckenham: Why then faith justifies not, nor saves not.

Jane: Yes, verily, faith (as St. Paul says) only [alone] justifies.

Feckenham: Why St. Paul says: If I have all faith without love, it is nothing.

Jane: True it is, for how can I love him in whom I trust not? Or how can I trust in him whom I love not? Faith and love agree both together, and yet love is comprehended in faith.

Feckenham: How shall we love our neighbor?

Jane: To love our neighbor is to feed the hungry, clothe the naked and give drink to the thirsty, and to do to Him as we would do to ourselves.

Feckenham: Why then is it necessary to salvation to do good works and it is not sufficient to believe?

Jane: I deny that and I affirm that faith only [alone] saves. But it is meet for Christians, in token that they follow their master Christ, to do good works, yet may we not say that they profit to salvation. For, although we have all done all that we can, yet we be unprofitable servants, and the faith only in Christ's blood saveth.

Feckenham: How many sacraments be there?

Jane: Two; the one the sacrament of baptism, and the other the sacrament of our Lord's supper.

Feckenham: No, there be seven.

Jane: By what Scripture find you that?

Feckenham: Well, we will talk thereof hereafter. But what is signified by your two sacraments?

Jane: By the sacrament of baptism, I am washed with water and regenerated by the Spirit; and that washing is a token to me that I am the child of God. The sacrament of the Lord's supper is offered unto me as a sure seal and testimony that I am by the blood of Christ, which He shed for me on the Cross, made partaker of the everlasting kingdom.

Feckenham: Why, what do you receive in that bread? Do you not receive the very body and blood of Christ?

Jane: No surely, I do not believe so. I think that at that supper I receive neither flesh nor blood, but only bread and wine. The which bread when it is broken, and the wine when it is drunk, put me in mind, how that for my sins the body of Christ was broken and His blood shed on the cross; and, with that bread and wine, I received the benefits that came by [the] breaking of His body and the shedding of His blood on the cross for my sins.

Feckenham: Why, doth not Christ speak these words: "Take, eat, this is my body?" Require we any plainer words? Doth not He say that it is His body?

Jane: I grant He says so, and so He says: "I am the vine, I am the door," but yet He is never the more the vine nor door. Doth not St. Paul say that He calleth those things that are not as though they were? God forbid that I should say that I eat the very natural body and blood of Christ, for then either I should pluck away my redemption, either else there were two bodies, or two Christs or else two bodies? The one body was tormented on the cross; . . . then, if they did eat another body, . . . either He had two bodies, [or] else, if His body [was] eaten, it was not broken upon the cross; . . . if it were broken upon the cross, it was not eaten [by] His disciples.

Feckenham: Why is it not as possible that Christ by His power could make His body both to be eaten and broken, as to be born of a woman without the seed of man, and as to walk on the sea, having a body, and other such like miracles as He wrought by His power only?

Jane: Yes, verily, if God would have done at His supper a miracle, He might have done so; but I say He minded no work or miracle but only to break His body and shed His blood on the cross for our sins. But I pray you answer me to this one question, Where was Christ when He said: "Take, eat, this is my body"? Was He not at the table when He said so? He was at that time alive, and suffered not till the next day. Well what took He but bread? And what break He but bread? And what gave He, but bread? Look what He took, He break; and look what He break, He gave; and look what He gave, that did they eat; and yet all this while He Himself was at supper before His disciples, or else they were deceived.

Feckenham: You ground your faith upon such authors as say and unsay, both with [one] breath, and not upon the church to whom you ought to give credit.

Jane: No, I ground my faith upon God's Word and not upon the church. For if the church be a good church, the faith of the church must be tried by God's Word, and not God's Word by the church, neither yet my faith. Shall I believe the church because of antiquity? Or shall I give credit to that church that taketh away from me that half part of the Lord's supper, and will let no laymen receive it in both hands but themselves? Which thing if they deny to us, they deny us part of our salvation; and I say that is an evil church, and not the spouse of Christ but the spouse of the devil, that alters the Lord's supper, and both taketh from it and addeth to it. To that church I say God will add plagues, and from that church will He take their part out of the Book of Life. Do you not learn that of St. Paul, when he ministered it to the Corinthians in both kinds? shall I believe that church? God forbid.

Feckenham: That was done of a good intent of the church to avoid an heresy that sprang [within] it.

Jane: Why, shall the church alter God's will and ordinances for a good intent? How did King Saul the Lord define? With these and such like persuasions, he [Feckenham] would have had me . . . lean to the church, but it would not be. There were many more things whereof we reasoned, but these were the chief.

By me,
Jane Dudley

7. Elizabethan Settlement: The Act of Supremacy, 1559

With the accession to the throne of Queen Elizabeth I (1558-1603) England became the leading Protestant nation. At the very outset of her long and glorious reign she undertook to secure the unity of the nation by arranging a religious settlement which has lasted through the subsequent centuries. She disliked both Catholicism and radical sectarian Protestantism and chose rather the *via media* of an Anglican establishment with an episcopal form of church government. In doctrine and discipline authority was to rest with King and parliament with the consent of the Convocation of the clergy. The Act of Supremacy, passed in January, 1559, repealed the Heresy Act of Philip and Mary, restored the Acts of King Henry VIII including the Acts on Annates and Appeals, and renewed the claims of the crown to supremacy over the church in England. From Henry Gee and William Hardy, *Documents Illustrative of English Church History* (London: Macmillan and Co., 1896), pp. 446-449.

And to the intent that all usurped and foreign power and authority, spiritual and temporal, may forever be clearly extinguished, and never . . . be used or obeyed within this realm or any other [of] your majesty's dominions or countries, may it please your highness that it may be further enacted by the authority aforesaid that no foreign prince, person, prelate, state or potentate, spiritual or temporal, shall at any time after the last day of this session of Parliament use, enjoy or exercise any manner of power, jurisdiction, superiority, authority, pre-eminence or privilege, spiritual or ecclesiastical, within this realm or within any other your majesty's dominions or countries that now be or hereafter shall be; but from thenceforth the same shall be clearly abolished out of this realm, and all other your highness' dominions forever; any statute, ordinance, custom, constitutions, or any other matter or cause whatsoever to the contrary in anywise notwithstanding.

And that also it may likewise please your highness that it may be established and enacted by the authority aforesaid, that such jurisdictions, privileges, superiorities and pre-eminences, spiritual and ecclesiastical, as by any spiritual or ecclesiastical power or authority have heretofore been, or may lawfully be exercised or used for the visitation of the ecclesiastical state and persons, and for reformation, order and correction of the same, and of all manner of errors, heresies, schisms, abuses, offences, contempts and enormities, shall forever, by authority of this present Parliament, be united and annexed to the imperial crown of this realm. . . .

And for the better observation and maintenance of this Act, may it please your highness that it may be further enacted by the authority aforesaid that all and every archbishop, bishop, and all and every other ecclesiastical person, and other ecclesiastical officer and minister, of what estate, dignity, pre-eminence, or degree soever he or they be or shall be, and all and every temporal judge, justice, mayor, and other lay or temporal officer and minister, and every other person having your highness's fee or wages, within this realm or any [of] your highness's dominions, shall make, take and receive a corporal oath upon the evangelist, before such person or persons as shall please your highness, your heirs or successors, under the great seal of England to assign and name, to accept and to take the same according to the tenor and effect hereafter following, that is to say:

"I, *A.B.*, do utterly testify and declare in my conscience that the queen's highness is the only supreme governor of this realm, and of all other [of] her highness's dominions and countries, as well in all spiritual or ecclesiastical things or causes as temporal, and that no foreign prince, person, prelate, state or potentate, has, or ought to have, any jurisdiction, power, superiority, pre-eminence or authority ecclesiastical or spiritual within this realm; and therefore I do utterly renounce and forsake all foreign jurisdictions, powers, superiorities and authorities, and do promise that from henceforth I shall bear faith and true allegiance to the queen's highness, her heirs and lawful successors, and to my power shall assist and defend all jurisdictions, pre-eminences, privileges and authorities granted or belonging to the queen's highness, her heirs and successors, or united and annexed to the imperial crown of this realm. So help me God, and by the contents of this book."

8. Elizabethan Settlement: The Act of Uniformity, 1559

Immediately after the passage of the Act of Supremacy, Parliament passed the Act of Uniformity. This reestablished Edward VI's *Book of Common Prayer* with some alterations and additions and determined a uniform practice in the rites and ceremonies, in prayer, and in the administration of the sacraments in the Church of England. Stringent penalties for violations were prescribed. The spiritual peers in the House of Lords voted against it and it was not submitted to the Convocation of the clergy, but it became the law of the land. The following selection is taken from Henry Gee and William Hardy, *Documents Illustrative of English Church History* (London: Macmillan and Co., 1896), pp. 458-459, 463, 467.

Where at the death of our late sovereign lord King Edward VI there remained one uniform order of common service and prayer, and of the administration of sacraments, rites and ceremonies in the Church of England, which was set forth in one book, [entitled]: *The Book of Common Prayer, and Administration of Sacraments, and other rites and ceremonies in the Church of England*; authorized by Act of Parliament [held] in the fifth and sixth years of our said late sovereign lord King Edward VI [entitled]: *An Act for the uniformity of common prayer, and administration of the sacraments*; the which was repealed and taken away by Act of Parliament in the first year of the reign of our late sovereign lady Queen Mary, to the great decay of the due honor of God and discomfort to the professors of the truth of Christ's religion:

Be it therefore enacted by the authority of this present Parliament that the said statute of repeal and everything therein contained, only concerning the said book, and the service, administration of sacraments, rites and ceremonies contained or appointed in or by the said book, shall be void and of none effect, from and after the feast of the Nativity of St. John Baptist next coming; and that the said book, with the order of service and of the administration of sacraments, rites and ceremonies, with the alterations and additions therein added and appointed by this statute, shall stand and be, from and after the said feast of the Nativity of St. John Baptist, in full force and effect, according to the tenor and effect of this statute; anything in the aforesaid statute of repeal to the contrary notwithstanding.

And further be it enacted by the queen's highness, with the assent of the Lords [sic] and Commons in this present Parliament assembled, and by authority of the same, that all and singular ministers in any cathedral or parish church, or other place within this realm of England, Wales and the marches of the same, or other [of] the queen's dominions, shall from and after the feast of the Nativity of St. John Baptist next coming be bounden to say and use the matins, evensong, celebration of the Lord's supper and administration of each of the sacraments, and all their common and open prayer, in such order and form as is mentioned in the said book, so authorized by Parliament in the said fifth and sixth years of the reign of King Edward VI; with one alteration or addition of certain lessons to be used on every Sunday in the year, and the form of the Litany altered and corrected, and two sentences only added in the delivery of the sacrament to the communicants, and none other or otherwise. . . .

And for due execution hereof, the queen's most excellent majesty, the Lords temporal [sic] and all the Commons, in this present

Parliament assembled, do in God's name earnestly require and charge all the archbishops, bishops and other ordinaries that they shall endeavor themselves to the uttermost of their knowledges, that the due and true execution hereof may be had throughout their dioceses and charges, as they will answer before God, for such evils and plagues wherewith Almighty God may justly punish His people for neglecting this good and wholesome law. . . .

And be it further enacted by the authority aforesaid that all laws, statutes and ordinances, wherein or whereby any other service, administration of sacraments or common prayer is limited, established or set forth to be used within this realm or any other [of] the queen's dominions or countries, shall from henceforth be utterly void and of none effect.

Reading List

A selection of works mostly available in English paperback editions

Anderson, Marvin W., The Battle for the Gospel: The Bible and the Reformation 1444-1589. Lexington, MA: Ginn Press, 1987.

Bainton, Roland H., Here I Stand: A Life of Martin Luther. New York: The New American Library, 1955.

Bainton, Roland H., Women of the Reformation: 3 vols. Minneapolis: Augsburg, 1971, 1973, 1977.

Bainton, Roland, and Gritsch, Eric W., Bibliography of the Continental Reformation. Hamden, CT: Archon Books, 1972.

Baker, J. Wayne, Heinrich Bullinger and the Covenant: The Other Reformed Tradition. Athens, OH: Ohio University Press, 1980.

Bouwsma, William J., John Calvin: A Sixteenth Century Portrait: New York and Oxford: Oxford University Press, 1988.

Brecht, Martin, Martin Luther: His Road to Reformation 1483-1521. Philadelphia: Fortress Press, 1981.

Buck, Lawrence P. and Zophy, Jonathan W., eds., The Social History of the Reformation. Columbus: Ohio State University Press, 1972.

Chadwick, Owen, The Reformation. Baltimore: Penguin Books, 1964.

Clark, Sir George, Early Modem Europe from about 1450 to about 1720. New York: Oxford University Press, 1960.

Davis, Natalie Zemon, Society and Culture in Early Modern France. Stanford, California: Stanford University Press, 1975.

Dickens, A. G., The English Reformation. London: 1964.

Dickens, A. G., and Tonkins, John, The Reformation in Historical Thought. Cambridge, MA: Harvard University Press, 1985.

Dickens, A. G., Martin Luther and the German Nation. New York: Harper & Row, 1974.

Dillenberger, John, ed., John Calvin: Selections from His Writings. Missoula, MT: Scholar's Press, 1971.

Dillenberger, John, ed., Martin Luther: Selections from His Writings. Garden City, N. Y.: Doubleday & Co., Inc.,

Dolan, John, P., ed., The Essential Erasmus. New York: The New American Library, 1964.

Ebeling, Gerhard, Luther: An Introduction to His Thought. Philadelphia: Fortress Press, 1972.

Edwards, Mark U., Jr., Luther and the False Brethren. Stanford, CA: Stanford University Press, 1975.

Edwards, Mark U., Jr., Luther's Last Battles: Politics and Polemics. 1531-46. Ithaca, NY: Cornell University Press, 1983.

Elton, G. R., ed., The New Cambridge Modem History. II. The Reformation 1520-1559. Cambridge: Cambridge University Press, 1958.

Friesen, Abraham, Reformation and Utopia: The Marxist Interpretation of the Reformation and Its Antecedents. Wiesbaden, Germany: Franz Steiner Verlag GmbH, 1974.

Gerrish, B. A., The Old Protestantism and the New: Essays on the Reformation Heritage. Chicago: University of Chicago Press, 1982.

Goertz, Hans-Jurgen, ed., Profiles of Radical Reformers: Biographical Sketches from Thomas Muntzer to Paracelsus. Kitchener, Ontario: Herald Press, 1982.

Goodman, Anthony and MacKay, Angus, eds., The Impact of Humanism on Western Europe. London and New York: Longman, 1990.

Graham, W. Fred, The Constructive Revolutionary: John Calvin and His Socio-Economic Impact: East Lansing, Michigan: Michigan State University Press, 1987.

Greyerz, Kaspar von, ed., Religion and Society in Early Modem Europe 1500-1800. London: George, Allen & Unwin, 1984.

Gritsch, Eric W., Martin—God's Court Jester: Luther in Retrospect. Philadelphia: Fortress Press, 1983.

Haile, H. G., Luther: An Experiment in Biography. Garden City, NY: Doubleday & Co., Inc., 1980.

Harbison, E. Harris, The Christian Scholar in the Age of Reformation. New York: Charles Scribner's Sons, 1956.

Harran, Marilyn J., ed., Luther and Learning. Selinsgrove, PA: Susquehanna University Press, 1984.

Harran, Marilyn J., Luther and Conversion: The Early Years. Ithaca, NY: Cornell University Press, 1983.

Hillerbrand, Hans J., The World of the Reformation. New York: Charles Scribner's Sons, 1973.

Hoffman, Manfred, ed., Martin Luther and the Modem Mind: Freedom, Conscience. Toleration Rights. New York: The Edwin Mellen Press, 1985.

Kittelson, James J., Luther the Reformer: The Story of the Man and His Career. Minneapolis: Augsburg Publishing House, 1986.

Kittelson, James M., Wolfgang Capito from Humanist to Reformer. Leiden: E. J. Brill, 1975.

Kingdon, Robert M., Geneva and the Coming of the Wars of Religion in France 1555-1563. Geneva: Droz, 1956.

Kingdon, Robert M., Geneva and the Consolidation of the French Protestant Movement 1564-1572. Madison, WI: The University of Wisconsin Press, 1967.

Lienhard, Marc, Luther: Witness to Jesus Christ: Stages and

Themes of the Reformer's Christology. Minneapolis: Augsburg Publishing House, 1982.

Jones, Rufus M., Spiritual Reformers in the 16th and 17th Centuries. Boston: Beacon Press, 1959.

McNeill, John T., The History and Character of Calvinism. New York: Oxford University Press, 1954.

Moeller, Bernd, Imperial Cities and the Reformation: Three Essays. Philadelphia: Fortress Press, 1972. (repr. Labyrinth Press)

Nauert, Charles, Jr., The Age of Renaissance and Reformation. Hinsdale, IL.: The Dryden Press, 1977.

Olivier, Daniel, Luther's Faith: The Cause of the Gospel in the Church. St. Louis, MO: Concordia Publishing House, 1982.

Olson, Jeannine E., Calvin and Social Welfare: Deacons and the Bourse Française. Selinsgrove, PA: Susquehanna University Press, 1989.

Ozment, Steven, The Age of Reform 1250-1550: An Intellectual and Religious History of Late Medieval and Reformation Europe. New Haven: Yale University Press, 1980.

Powicke, Sir Maurice, The Reformation in England. London: Oxford University Press, 1961.

Rupp, E. Gordon, Luther's Progress to the Diet of Worms. New York: Harper & Row, 1964.

Smith, Preserved, Erasmus. New York: Dover Publications, 1962.

Spitz, Lewis W., The Protestant Reformation 1517-1559. New York: Harper & Row, 1985.

Spitz, Lewis W., The Reformation - Basic Interpretations. Lexington, MA: D. C. Heath and Company, 1972.

Spitz, Lewis W., The Renaissance and Reformation Movements, 2 vols. St. Louis, MO: Concordia Publishing House, 2 ed., 1987.

Tawney, R. H., <u>Religion and the Rise of Capitalism</u>. New York: The New American Library, 1947.

Weber, Max, <u>The Protestant Ethic and the Spirit of Capitalism</u>. New York: Charles Scribner's Sons, 1958.

Weisner, Merry E., <u>Women in the Sixteenth Century</u>. St. Louis, Mo.: Center for Reformation Research, 1983.

Whale, J. S., <u>The Protestant Tradition</u>. Cambridge: The University Press, 1962.

Williams, George H., <u>The Radical Reformation</u>. Cambridge, MA: Harvard University Press, 1962.

Williams, George H., ed., <u>Spiritual and Anabaptist Writers: Documents Illustrative of the Radical Reformation</u>. Philadelphia: The Westminster Press, 1957.

Zwingli, Ulrich, <u>Ulrich Zwingli 1484-1531: Selected Works</u>. Philadelphia: The University of Pennsylvania Press, 1972.